The First Four Books of Sampson Starkweather

BIRDS, LLC | AUSTIN, MINNEAPOLIS, NEW YORK, RALEIGH

Birds, LLC
Austin, Minneapolis, New York, Raleigh
www.birdsllc.com

Cover art by Matt Bollinger
Interior art by Bianca Stone, Eric Amling, Jonathan Marshall, Sommer Browning
Interior designed by Michael Newton

Library of Congress Cataloging-in-Publication Data:
Starkweather, Sampson
The First Four Books of Sampson Starkweather/Sampson Starkweather
Library of Congress Control Number: 2012918911

First Edition, 2013
ISBN-13: 9780982617793
Printed in the United States of America

CONTENTS

INTRODUCTION

In his introduction to the poems of Guillaume Apollinaire, Roger Shattuck writes about a central "heresy" of literary personas: the separation of the lives of the poet into "his biography, his myth, his verse." "Where they all coincide," writes Shattuck, "is the area which we can most unmistakably identify as the poet." To read a book of poems, then, is not merely to approach the words on the page or the story of a life, but to enter a mythology.

Holding in your hands *The First Four Books of Sampson Starkweather* necessarily begs the question, who is Sampson Starkweather? What sort of poet publishes not merely a single book but four, a gesture that could as easily imply hubris or extravagance as exuberance and flair? We live in an era when a book of poems is often a 50-80 page manuscript bound with a thin mustache of spine. Thick volumes of Selected Poems or collections of books bound together wait for the mid-late career poet printed as loss-leader by a publishing conglomerate (we expect, say, the First Four Books of W.S. Merwin or John Ashbery).

Legally speaking, Birds, LLC is indeed a corporation but only in a playful, beat-em-at-their-own-game kind of way, and, as one of the poet founders of the press, Sampson Starkweather is in a perfect position to upend this orthodoxy by punching his own ticket, writing his own myth. There's a wonderful German term for a certain kind of coming-of-age narrative in which the hero becomes a writer: künstlerroman. Think of Joyce's *Portrait of the Artist as a Young Man*, or Goethe's *The Sorrows of Young Werther*, or Rilke's *Notebooks of Malte Laurids Brigge*—tales of suffering self-imposed by the rigorous loneliness of the writing process. *The First Four Books of Sampson Starkweather* is no less than this: a book of books about the lonely yearning to be transformed by poetry, and through poetry to transform the world. Over the course of these four books, Starkweather's poems coalesce to form the outlines of a novel whose subject is a poet making up himself.

For several years when the poems in these books first began to appear online and in poetry journals, Starkweather's biographical notes would come full of fantastical grace notes and tongue-in-cheek pledges building to a climax: "He lives in the woods alone." Like so many claims that sound like fictions, this happened to be 100% accurate—he did in fact live in a cottage by himself in a valley in Westchester County, New York. At the same time, he was also teasing a persona and a whole set of preoccupations: the enfant terrible-cowboy-hermit-grizzled-fighter-lover poet, turning loneliness, violence and desire into macho art in an empty room with a typewriter and a bottle of whisky, writing poetry equal parts camaraderie and aggression and slowly vanishing into jungles real or imaginary. Rimbaud in Africa, Brautigan in Montana, Lorca in New York, Jack Nicholson in the Overlook Hotel. This is a mural that includes Wallace Stevens fistfighting Ernest Hemingway in Key West, Ezra Pound madly striking through lines to edit *The Wasteland*, a poetry of equal parts aggression and cama-raderie, wishes and bull. Starkweather puns at one point about mishearing the classic modernist city of Brasilia as "Brah-zilla," a man-jock avatar, fraternity athlete blown up to absurd Godzilla proportions. This is not aggrandizement, but subversion. By making his home "in the woods alone," Starkweather invokes this mantle of epic maleness so flatly that it becomes an absurd-sounding exaggeration, a space to play inside and tear apart, an empty, haunted suit of armor.

Mythology is complicated, because it can so easily become a lens that distorts, ennobling pointless suffering, erasing victims, replacing lived experience with stereotypes and imagos, stuffed corpses mistaken for heroes. Starkweather is hip to these risks, as when he suggests, "I'm pretty sure the things that kill you make you stronger too." These poems interest themselves in the purity of experience, everything being something that will never happen again. They mine dreams, threads of hope. Starkweather has spoken about his reverence for the dreamlife—his own and that of others, and he returns frequently to this wellspring of creativity. Dreaming is in a certain sense a scandal hiding in plain sight: the universal unacknowledged capacity for creativity, the power of the imagination. In dreams, as in poems, one can survive one's own death.

So if a book is an afterlife, why not have four? For these are indeed four separate books with their own forms and voices and preoccupations. *King of the Forest*—the title cleverly unites Jack Spicer's wounded language lion with the title of one of fugitive novelist Benno von Archimboldi's titles in Roberto Bolaño's *2666*—works in prose with the material of dreams, phantasmal geographies and the sudden appearance of magical children, ghosts of childhood. *La La La* fractures syllogisms, turning them inside out and reworking them into bass-voiced sexy soul-singer slow jams. *The Waters* steps into the footprints of Cesar Vallejo's *Trilce*, gently inviting this paradigmatic work of modernist poetry to haunt a latter-day homage that is not a translation but, Starkweather instead suggests, a 'transcon-temporation.' Residue of Vallejo—words rummaged through and arrayed like broken bits of stone—remain like a mineral deposit swirled into these poems that record the experience of a confrontation, a dialogue between ghosts. Bringing this passionate late-into-the-night conversation fully into the present, *Self Help Poems* transfigures email dispatches into an exploration of poem-friendship and wounded, punch-drunk Harlequin-Robocop masculinity.

Disparate but kindred, these books are like four ecologically distinct quadrants of one realm, attractions in a Disneyland of poetry's possibilities. Each is a serial poem, a long poem made of smaller poems, sometimes with even smaller poems hiding within them. Poetic strategies recur—the figurative taken literally, mishearings elevated into symbols, words rooted out from inside words (like the "word" in "sword")—as, looking closer, the four books multiply into many, an infinite nested structure of books within books within books. "Kudzu in the Garden of Eden," Starkweather writes in the "City of Moths" section of

King of the Forest, a wonderful metaphor for this overgrown book of books, celebrating grandiosity of gesture, obsession, excess, heartbreak, melodrama, raw open-hearted emotion. The poems clown and crack and rage as, like *The Cantos of Ezra Pound*, they become voluminous museums of the varieties of contemporary language. News reports, video games, WWF wrestling, Mike Tyson: this is a phantasmagoria worthy of Arthur Rimbaud but a "Rimbaud chugging Robitussin®," as Starkweather writes in an over-the-top yoking of high and low, language of belief and cynical branding. It's a gag but it is also somehow perfect, because if Rimbaud really were a teenager today, wouldn't he be a teenage Robo-tripper…and yet still somehow writing the poems of Arthur Rimbaud?

This quip-logic of unstable prophecy holds sway as trees fall in Starkweather's woods and keep falling. Maybe the poet alone hears them or maybe—the thought occurs more than once—the poet *is* the tree that makes or does not make a sound. Starkweather loves to dig into such tropes and truisms, suggesting that, contrary to the old saw about waiting for the other shoe to drop, that "there is no other shoe, only the one we already have, and waiting." Starkweather invokes the 8-bit landscapes of Super Mario Brothers, its urban pastoral pipes and hammers and ravines and mushroom-leaps that the artist Cory Arcangel memorably erased, leaving behind an elegy made only of sky and wisps of digital clouds. It is this sublimity that can be found in *The First Four Books of Sampson Starkweather*: the sublime and the "ridonculous."

A solitary voice calls into a void: "When I walk out into the dark, I feel I'm going to be pulled in and mauled by some creature. I'm practically waiting for it. When my motion light goes on, I know some animal is approaching." These poems live at the far edge of reality, because poetry thrives on truth but "has no pretensions of being real, it doesn't care if you believe, it doesn't even believe in itself, it *is*, or it is just…language." Picking up Vallejo's cubist neologism "odumodneurtse!"—mute roar spelled backwards in Spanish—Starkweather brings his own talisman, "rudderowstarkweathersampson!": the poet both sculler and vessel, setting a course through an ocean that is also a forest toward a land where he is king.

As his *First Four Books* arrive, Sampson Starkweather no longer lives in the woods. He is not alone. These poems are with him. These books, his friends. We join him as we read. Now we are alone. We live in the woods.

Jared White
Brooklyn
January, 2013

3

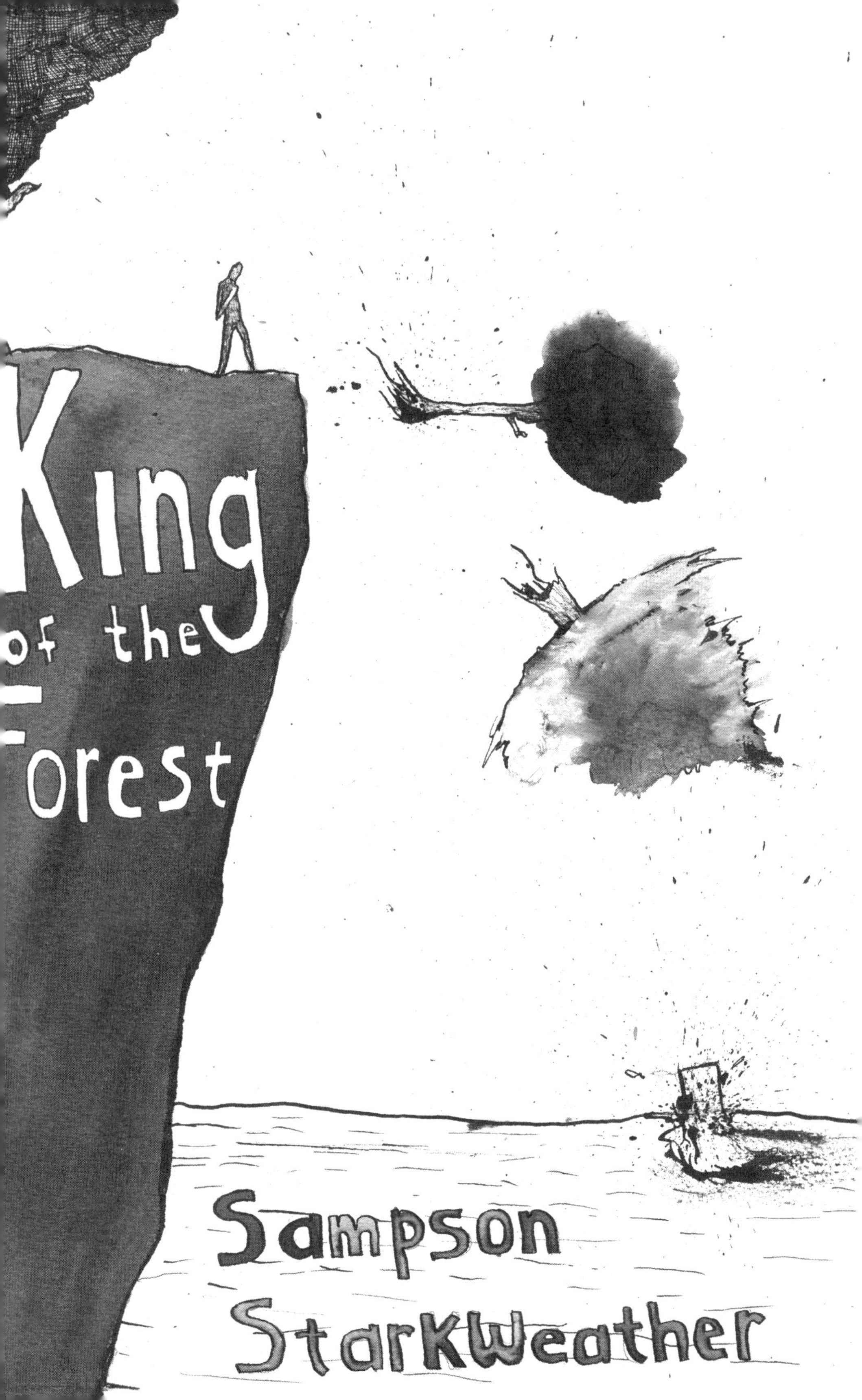
King
of the
Forest
Sampson
Starkweather

KING OF

THE FOREST †

SAMPSON

STARKWEATHER

Look I am King Of The Forest
Says The King Of The Forest
As he growls magnificently
Look, I am in pain. My right leg
Does not fit my left leg.
I am King Of The Forest
Says The King Of The Forest.
And the other beasts hear him and would rather
They were King Of The Forest
But that their right leg
Would fit their left leg.
'Beauty is so rare a thing,' Pound sang.
'So few drink at my fountain.'

~Jack Spicer,
"II" from *Fifteen False Propositions Against God*

i. City of Moths

THERE ARE CONSTANTLY packs of wolves in the city wandering around abandoned monuments and subway stations without any sense of fear or resistance. As long as you mind your own business, they too will ignore you. But should some tourist acknowledge their existence or a young girl, sensing their animal presence, make a sharp movement, they will immediately swarm the victim, and with their razor claws and teeth, tear the person to pieces before devouring them in public. It's hard to pretend the shrieks are not happening, but most people are trained by now to drown out the sounds. I should remind you that most of the time they simply walk through the city, peacefully, with nothing at all to do.

I know you need the city but we all have our forests. A place for things to grow or fail...to go unnoticed. A place for things to fall. I am speaking of the heart. I'm not ashamed...to talk about the weather. With you, it's more than small talk because you told me how the sky laid down when your grandmother died. Some wind that sounded like an army blew through my backyard. I was told, a tornado almost. I was so absorbed in my war I didn't even notice the storm. All these aftermaths, one can barely recall the befores. Have you ever stood in the woods, seen a downed tree? It reminds me of blind-deaf people who define themselves by what they've touched. On the other hand, there's what touches us. The scattered seeds of these aftermaths. What will grow or what's destined to be downed. They remind me of you. The trees in the trees.

Somewhere in *Poet in New York*, Lorca says *agony, agony, dream, ferment and dream. That's the way of the world my friend, agony, agony*. A ratio, that's all. Human geometry. The shortest distance between any two points (peoples' lives) is a straight lie. The body is an obsolete barometer. In the city, yours can't help but be touched. I have these dead bees in my bathtub, which is what Lorca meant by ferment. Things change. Remember that winged-thing we stopped to look at in the snow: *What a burning angel I look for and am*. I was meaning to tell you, I had this dream last night, but I barely remember anything, just that there was wind, and it was green.

If a man falls in a forest and no one is around, does he still make a sound? And how the hell is a Swiss army knife supposed to save you? Nature follows the same laws as art. Or language. The zoo we all lose our nature to. The line between being made or being born. Usefulness vs. Beauty. There is no difference between a poem and a tree. A crooked tree has no responsibility. My friend doesn't know if he believes in God or not, which itself is an art. Shelly says the great mystery of morals is love. The book I'm reading says "*God-sin-holiness*-are." I am deathly afraid of the IRS and falling in a forest with no one around. But I guess you know that by now. As for that army knife, *Whatever threatens us with destruction is hidden within, to let the self be annihilated right down to some last atom, from the resistance of which will grow—a world* is what I carved into the tree of me.

This is the story of dark matter. One Saturday morning a 6-year-old girl walked right into my cottage. When I woke, she was standing at the foot of the bed, and said, "This used to be my dollhouse." A pact, unmentioned, fledged. Sometimes I see her on the swings or hear her playing in the trees. She knows you are gone, but for me will make-believe.

My friend thinks that poetry has nothing to do with words. Poetry she says, is a mountain. An actual mountain. A thing that fools climb simply "because it's there." Poetry is there, but why do we constantly feel the need to prove it exists? To point to it? Like a mountain appearing in the distance. "Be an uncarved block of wood" is what the Sarah Lawrence kids, who hadn't slept in 40-some hours, still high on ecstasy and acid, sitting Indian-style on the rock, otherwise-silent, would shout at me during tennis matches. They were right. What lies in the uncarved block of wood. Whorls and grains, stories and held smoke. Surrounded by. My block of wood, another person's mountain. The sound of a finger pointing to some unseen thing. To be reckoned with, or perhaps, reckoned by. Something to draw a door in.

I believe in scarecrows. They're more convincing than people and much less frightening. Which explains why I fell in love with one. In the sixth grade, my class went on a field trip to a factory in North Carolina where they manufactured scarecrows. Bright effigies hanging in rows from the ceiling. I thought fire. And that was that.

You can have your fucking city back. Just writing that feels like confessing a sin. Do you ever feel that guilt is our religion? I used to tell my mom, "My religion is that I love you." Foolish boy, king of straw. Don't tell anyone, but some of the scarecrows made a mistake and were real.

Your exercises in empathy are encouraging, but is it really possible for two people to ever understand each other? Useless as a mirror on the inside. Exercises, huh? If you could be me…but isn't this the principle of poetry—okay—magic, the illusion we can change? Things don't change. We just fold to time, simple physics. Your seasons, your rhythms, your tides, your laws: I feel these things…working against me. You are a genius for leaving me.

Sometimes, like right now, when snow has muted the world, I can hear the sound of your sadness, a small bird flailing in the grass, one wing making a useless music, and sometimes circumstance is the victim. There are certain silences only those who have suffered can know, what Coleridge called "the secret ministries of frost." They make a lake between us, an untouchable body. Misunderstanding is more than a language we've mastered—it's a life. This will go on until there is no more ground between us, until we're entwined in incessant falling. Things break. This is the first law of any beauty. Gravity. The way islands are made. I am the list of things you will break. I'm not really trying to tell you anything; I just wanted you to hear the sound of being alone, oh yeah, and the snow is deep and bright.

Poetry is exactly like sexual harassment. Don't ask. Listening to James Brown, I understood what you meant about poetry having nothing to do with words. Maybe my mountain is a woman...lying... down. *Try me*, a bridge, the black lightning of the body. Point to point, nearness to nearness, the point is always to get to the next poem. That's it. Nothing else. There's love, but either way, you end up going crazy. Maybe if this was music you would feel it, and you would understand. It's the language that gets in the way. What I'm really trying to say is, *Please, please, please...don't leave me...be...wildered.*

Now I'm writing to you from inside your left lung, which, being slightly smaller than your right lung, makes room for your heart. Sometimes you breathe more convincingly, and at the repose of your more harmonious lung, the entire world rises in your chest, a wave on the precipice of a kiss. I feel like an ocean in here, tossed around and constantly crashing, but I'm more of a minor body, like an 8th unacknowledged sea. You should really come see what it's like down here, to be me. So many vibrant fires raving and playing truant in my troubled water. The debris of this sea—my smoldering desire. And you go on breathing normally.

Human beings are weird. We have words for words. Ways to say things to make sense of all this suffering. The only thing that can diffuse a nuclear bomb is a new vocabulary. The perfect poem you can walk inside of and watch yourself from above on a series of TVs. A city above the city. An architecture of sound. Real poetry is a gesture without words. A little girl in the grass, kneeling. A gun. A thousand ways to say, *God*.

As for suffering, didn't the old masters realize how boring it is? Maybe if they made it personal. When I told you *you will suffer for the rest of your life*, how could I have known that I meant it? And this bores even me. Maybe if there were wolves. Or accounts of certain sexual positions. The truth is everyone loves to see someone suffer, and the truth is *long you must suffer, not knowing what, until suddenly, from an apple hatefully bitten, the taste of suffering enters you. And then you already almost love what you've savored. No one will talk it out of you again.*

Every sentence is a certain surrender. Our lines, like our loves, are without loyalty or affiliation, simply satisfied with lying the way they were born into. Is that really the end…of the sentence? I wanted to be a robot-cop, until the scene when the politician did all that blow off the blonde's tits on the rooftop of some city. Look what dreams lead to. All my lines and loves trying to survive on an island like *Lord of the Flies*. My flag isn't white, it's impossible.

In the myth I made, I was of course, the King, and had demanded by decree that only I should slay my unfaithful Queen, but when I raised my sword to slay you, you let your robe slip from your shoulders. My sword dropped from my hand. Kudzu in the Garden of Eden. But we both knew who the fool was. Nothing is worthy of love. Absolutely.

Grass is merely an idea here. It was not always this way. But who's to blame? The pigeons shit on the living and the dead, regardless of God. There's something brave and beautiful about such stupidity. I have seen the panhandlers in the subway sing and dance and smile like the sun. And I am happier than you, and they are happier than I. And the pigeons in the square have wings and can barely even fly.

The Queen's relationship with the King varies depending on the source of the story. In some, she loved him dearly. In others, she was portrayed as his unwilling prisoner in the kingdom, or as a cruel, selfish woman who brought disaster to everyone around her. What we do know is in the summer they met, they were constantly surrounded by water. A blessing, a gift. But of course, it couldn't protect them from everything, unless, you think it really could protect them from everything?

Before we leave, there's one more thing I need to know. Do you still live in the city we made? I don't remember anything but rinsing your scent off my skin, or was it the source? Who's to say what is real? Was *that* what I loved? Or was it the open window so the whole world could see me naked and new? I suppose we'll never know. Tell me, what do you think, when you talk freely, without reservation, without fear, when you speak of me with your heart wide open, theoretically speaking obviously.

I am writing to you from the end of the world. You must realize this. The trees often tremble. We collect the leaves. They have an absurd amount of veins. But what for? There's nothing between them and the tree anymore, and we go off troubled. Could life continue without wind? Or must everything tremble, always, always? There is life underground too, stored up like a well, like angers which might make their way to meet us, or stern ghosts who are coming to strong-arm confessions. We see nothing, except what is so unimportant to see. Nothing, and yet we tremble. Why? Nothing, and yet we tremble. Why?

Yes, it's true, a city is made of human beings, buildings, and birds. Which would, in most cases, be enough for poetry. All that chittering to tune into. All that infrastructure of breath. But I come crawling in from the woods and like a stick seeking water, *assay what lives the dearest freshness deep down things.* My work is the night. You, in your room, looking up the word *thirst.* Beneath the city, rustling, a river of moths.

Things fit together. Two inconsequential things can combine together to become a consequence. The poem doesn't exist by itself. Likewise, our fears and desires, our angers and dreams are not unique, they relate, become one and like us, will die if left alone. Did I tell you I was watching Game 2 of the Playoffs between the Detroit Pistons and the Orlando Magic when suddenly there appeared on the screen this skinny little white boy with glasses, a Pistons fan, maybe ten years old, shirtless, standing in the aisle, flexing imaginary muscles, and painted on the entirety of his chest in glittery pink and blue spray-paint was the message, "There's No Such Thing As Magic" and POOF—you were beside me, naked and in my arms?

The more I become a block of wood, the more you grow into a mountain. *Asia Minor. Continental drift. String theory. Slip.* Words, you taught me, are as real as any lemon rind, as any bright nail. You would have painted them too, if I would have let you. If I'd say "blue," you'd see the sky and I'd see the sea. Words lodge between us. I'm breaking into an archipelago. Besides, you know how much I hate art, now hand me that hammer, ghost — and you call *that* gone?

I am *always* thinking about poetry, even when love smacks me down like a stunned bird. Which explains why I failed the fourth-grade, drawing battleships shooting unending sentences at invisible enemies. I invented my own dictionary; its first sentence was *Her rave tread me with o and Her be mother.* I gave names to my first thousand boners. Since the moment I met you, drunk, in a Mediterranean diner, I've always wanted to end a sentence *a grave and mysterious girl stunned by the beating of her own heart.* I mean anything's possible, right?

Wait, I have a question — Is a man, severed from his own shadow, covered by the Death and Dismemberment Plan? I only ask because I live in the forest, and lately light can't find its way through the pines. Okay, for the sake of full disclosure, I'm afraid a woman has split my heart like firewood. Take me off speaker-phone for a second. Can you speak to the third-party for me directly? Good, write this down: *Why does your love always feel like fumbling for condoms, as if it was your own fear that was fucking you? The way one enters the ocean with a simultaneous sense of both arrival and exile. Do you still pretend to love what you're afraid to love? The day you left you became a great white bird and the rain came like a forgotten promise. Now turn around and sail into your ultimatum.* I hope you're getting this all down.

Here, take this handgun, cradle it, be confident but don't think about what you are doing—point it at the heart of what you want to kill. Here are your perfect bullets, here is his fairytale trust. When the moment arrives, don't apologize for your anxiety, no, no, you are the doll-maker, the empress of holes, leave your name like a calling card. There's no treason as true as the holes you left. No season to help us heal. *Summer inside the two dolls has wound down.*

Drowning, it turns out, is not difficult. Bodies in deep water lie in complete darkness. *The ambiguous ambiguous.* One must learn to lose, because eventually everything runs past you and away from you. Like the minnows made angry at all we do. The dead often surface in spring. I am a flower. My name is doubled-over. "Weight," you say and that is the soul's only argument. And all the little fish wear white gloves and swim past us.

I am not a good person. Tell me I'm wrong. Tell me
we are the only two people in the world. That the
poem will end when we die. I apologize for the future.
Which is why I'm building a spaceship in the woods.
I am going on a journey where all possible outcomes
will end in fire. No need to wave when I fly over.
This time there will be no knock. I will enter you
through the door in your desire.

We remain, your absence and I. It turns out it was me that was making all that pink noise. Translating something so fragile there is no way to deny it wasn't *the whore of the invisible.* I didn't say, "something died inside me." The crows go crazy outside. Jealous of my black pool.

I write like I'm staring at a mountain. Waiting for
something red and too true to fall. I am afraid. I am
afraid of what I know and what I don't. Something
flees from me like frightened horses. Do you feel it?
I have this picture of you where something is escaping
and inside your eyes there are birds frozen in a Chinese
fan. You look as if you've just said something beautiful
or criminal. I cradle your apology in my hands to sip
from it.

For a long time now we have been at war with the sea. I can see how she must seem blue and at peace from an outside eye. But that's all advertising. The problem is that the sea is perceived with the wrong sense. Don't be fooled by the sound, she is actually noiseless. I should explain the matter of the waves, it's quite complicated but…you must comply. Would I lie to you? The sea is more than her names, or the sum of the fears and joys she invokes. She exists, I swear, I see her everywhere! She has been sent from somewhere far away to seduce and terrify. When you come you will see for yourself. We will walk together and look at her. We will take deep breaths of the salty air, and I am sure with you there, we won't be afraid.

This is one of those stories with a boy and a girl. Spark, chasm, spark. I swear nothing mattered after I watched you put on a white belt. More than we want, we want to know. *What is love like for you?* In war, when enemies speak different languages it is said to make the killing easier, as for love… This is one of those stories where no one survives.

The IRS is after me again. I mailed them Lorca's "The Ballad of Weeping" with my W-2. *Because there are very few angels who sing. Because there is room for a thousand violins in the palm of my hand.* These are the things I claimed: You know those cold black leaves that settle at the bottom of river beds? The mud that comes up between your toes? Remember the cusp of thunderstorm and my kiss against the ivy fence? Apparently, remembering is not enough.

The sea again? The problem is she is also afraid of the future. Whose condition shares the characters of water. We are animals of the conditional. We float belly-up. Streams and rivers flow forward, but not the sea. You see my dilemma? I wouldn't lie to you. Despite how excited she gets, she will always stop at the first sign of sand. Goddess of giving way. It's not the idea of the future, to reach the other side of desire—it is simply her lot. But you never know, maybe someday even the sea will flow forward.

More than ever we are surrounded by moths. They light on the ceiling, silent and still. They have no concern with the living. If touched, they burst into dust. And still nothing is moved. A loose society built on silence and reverie. *Every city forms its slums and the ghosts of it.* Even alone, they project schemes and blueprints — a filament-less infrastructure...they are among themselves, everywhere, always. And even at this white moment in which I write this, not one moth has moved. The first to be crushed.

The education of trembling is not handled well in this city. We lack a working knowledge of the rules, and when an occurrence arises in front of our eyes, no one notices. No one is moved. Some theories pin it to time. We must arrive slightly sooner than it does; always arriving a tiny bit ahead of the origin…of the chill. It's the same with love, you can kill all the winged things but never the source. You know the story of the moth in the drawer? Of course you do. And isn't it true. I don't know what more to say. Tell me, when are you coming home?

ii. The Photograph

Ask the photograph. It says science. It says spoon. It says you will not remember how black the sky was over the parking lot when you held her wrist as if it were sand. You can't "capture" a moment. All that light. A cage.

There is a process in photography called burning when a person or image is burned-out of the picture to get it just right. Memory's like that. The image as language. This has to do with mathematics. Or desire. Slowly losing out. Images turn up like the silver bellies of dead fish making an alphabet in the Hudson. In Canada, a girl falls off her bicycle and skins her knee. Love is not like riding a bicycle. From a bridge, the lack of beauty is impossible.

There is no feeling like fiddling with a camera. Each icon, the words for: moon, mountain, stars. We calculate their weight, appropriate postage. There is no longer a necessity to lick stamps. What happens to the words: shutter-speed, lens cap, flash. To deal with the undeliverable, the U.S. Postal Service started a dead letter office. The words don't die, people do. No one goes "postal" without a heart. Beat-beat. Beat-beat.

You believe in words. Their power. Weight. Like some kind of nerd. Words too can get inside you. Unprotected. Circumcision of silence. So you forwarded me an email with your subscribed-to word-of-the-day: Deflagrate: 1. to burn; *verb;* 2. Chiefly *Chem.* to burst into flames and burn away rapidly. Words are useless on their own. Build something. Jesus was a carpenter; this was the only thing the Bible got right. Love as a message is impossible. Love as a nail driven into heartwood pine is real. We live in the real.

When I say, "you," I don't mean you. The poem has two hearts. Tony Hoagland can do nothing about it. Everybody knows there's no such thing as the perfect poem. Music. I have burned you out of the poem to get it just right. Chemicals of the cursor. The perfect poem without you. The right lie. In the medical field, this is referred to as the position of the fetus. A nurse holding an ultrasound up to a wall of light. If an unborn child does not have the "right lie," there can be complications. *The human being is the only species that clambers to be lied to.* The doctors perform a procedure to rotate the fetus. The earth turning. A record of this. Human music.

When light has the same properties as water, it's known as the "right light." Flowing, beneath the ground. Imperfect, real. A girl can be perfect. A poem, like "you," is relegated to a brilliant almost. The back of a calf, a "relatively average" calf. Walking away. I told myself, if I couldn't have (hold: this has to do with ownership) her, I'd leave her with (my: this is the poet's "right lie") words. (Less messy) or maybe more, which might be nice. The same hotel. People check in and out. A used key-card in the parking lot. Number 356.

The photograph is proof of time. This has to do with "flaws" in god's plan. Watchmakers make mistakes too. Numbers vs. Images. Geometry as evidence against agony: Exhibit A: the shadow loses no blood. Photography is a footnote of light. No one reads books in the dark. The politics of light can get tricky. Abraham Lincoln knew this and so was shot—a spurt of shadow from the hole in his head. President Kennedy also came too close. A motorcade of light. In the home movie, you can make out a bloodbird fly from his neck, Jackie's face flooded in light. Hell is merely a series of images you can't shake. A hand, waving goodbye.

The poet must pay for making a private language in his poem. The soul proprietor. Back taxes. You can't invent a world out of language. Stupid poet. A keyboard of images. Fish. Seaweed. Around the heart. This has to do with how long you can hold your breath. Count to 70. The correct way to drown.

The photograph attempts to create a "flowing boundary" between the invisible and what Crane called "the bees of paradise." Rilke had his bees "of the invisible." Rimbaud in Africa, a footnote. In one photo, Rimbaud has a halo. A textbook of light. We edit into existence. A girl's leg disappearing. A hallway of possibility. A new Eurydice. A green dress stitched with light. On her shoulders by thin electricity. Pull the plug. The leg is flesh, which doesn't make it real. Eyes are out of the equation. Walls are real. It's in their nature, being that they divide. The Chinese have 3 and ½ years to figure out how to keep the rain out of the Olympics. This has to do with probability. A piano underwater in New Orleans. A photograph of music.

The photograph does not fade away ala *Back to the Future*. People do. Real people. Feel such things. Which doesn't make them real. Some Hollywood writer knew this metaphor would resonate with Americans. Having burned himself out of the photos of everyone he ever loved. Photographs are a product of acids. There is a dark room where the slow revelation of memory occurs, submerged in chemical water. The "lost" boa constrictor on a flyer stuck to a telephone pole in Pittsboro, NC. Disintegrating in southern rain.

A famous photographer went to India and gave cameras to the children of prostitutes. What she knew was that the photos that come closest to this world are all wrong. The right light. She taught them nothing. A form of perfection. A child's eye to get the feeling to come through. The world is out of focus. Some of the best shots were taken by a boy sitting on the handlebars of a bicycle. The winning photo was taking during a cartwheel by a 13-year-old girl who would become a prostitute the next year. Time defied by a cartwheel. A girl standing on her hands. Time: a commodity. A man in the street selling DVD's — *Back to the Future*, 400 rupees.

The "you" is boring. The actual you. But your calf in the photograph has nothing to do with you. Cropped out. Keats couldn't have known he was talking about desire when he came up with "negative capability." But his brother understood. A dead letter. An empty space in a crossword puzzle. Love is the longing for love. Nothing is delivered. Come rain, sleet, or snow.

Love or a Polaroid—the suspension of disbelief. Chemistry states belief is a suspension. Oil and water. Lips pressed against lips. Birds fall from the trees. Newtonian bullshit. A photograph has no bodily fluids. It cannot compete with the pleasures of salad dressing. It is not, to my knowledge, capable of flamenco dancing. A traveling darkroom. The positive peeled from the negative. Like all great inventions, the Polaroid was a product of a girl. Ask the grass. Ask the father "Why can't I see it now?" Love never stood a chance.

The photograph is a life/or has a life? Hölderlin says death too is a life. But Hölderlin never had his picture taken. He would have looked like lightning. A portrait of lightning. Everlasting. A photo is not unlike a body of water. Think of a way it's not and you have no imagination. A bridge. A rusted refrigerator by the tracks. A 1994 yearbook of clouds. The awkward teenage years. Pittsboro Thrift Shop, Tuesday, 12:30 AM, the pants section, acid-washed jeans, left back pocket. The little black teeth of a comb.

A girl's leg is not a girl's leg. The dress presently is made of common cloth, hanging like a ghost. Captured by a walk-in closet. It has no memory. Of being light. An image of an anti-image—night. We tread between. My uncle would walk into the night taking photos of what he couldn't see. A map of the desert. In math, there are equations that never end. The distance between Japanese beetles. 30% of all Americans have metal in their body. Magnets holding art to a refrigerator. I used to wonder what would happen if a plane flew through a rainbow. Skin is the largest organ. It's like Russia. Nobody realizes its size, the way you can die out there. Try waging a war within skin. History is a placemat. Labor movements are never remembered. The job of skin. *Popeye was righteous.* Everything is replaced. There is no face in the photograph.

The "you" wants to know what the poem knows about the photograph. A green dress. Falling. Like cotton off light's hips. The you wants the words. It wants to slide them in its back pocket like those flimsy black combs the schools gave out on "picture day." It wants its frame. Glory. Glory. The poem doesn't care about you. It wants you to get a nosebleed. It wants you to have serious underwear issues on Broadway and West 28th Street. A clock breathing. The poem's finger, trembling on a white rook. The you, gnawing off the black knight's head. The poem always has a handful of your pieces beside her, off the board, standing like little gravestones. A cemetery. Of you.

Old-fashioned cameras had a lens that showed the image upside down. This has to do with the machinery of the eye. And ice cream cones. The first cameras were built by biologists to mimic the human eye. To observe time objectively. The scientific method. Cage it like a yellow screeching bird. One theory says this was many people's definition of God during the Industrial Revolution. The book of the wrench. A machine eye that could "keep" time. This has to do with slavery. Thelonious Monk. Light inside a white key. A zoo of it. You can't keep it like a piece of the World Trade Center. Infomercial blues. Beauty uses you. Jinx.

In chemistry, there is a saying: *like dissolves like*. In photography, the saying goes: *The camera loves action*. They also say *the camera doesn't lie*, which of course is a lie. The wrong lie. The I. In the photograph there is no you, the girl is light. Beauty beyond the message. A leg. A dress. A walking away. Movement trailed by halos. The girl. Disappearing. Behind a wall. To each his own hand-stitched hell. One cannot "turn one's back." Ask Orpheus. But this has nothing to do with love. I have burned it out. The realms of heart to heart, forever. The you, in the photograph, becoming ash.

A photograph is a symbol. Of status, or an incantation of Christ. A farmer holding a pitchfork like a dream. The sheep slung over a man's shoulders. An idea of. Goodness. In an image, "the Other" is always implied. The one eye of a fish carved into a wall was the world's first camera. The fisher king. An advertisement. A powerful image is one you can't see. Light is simply a degree of darkness. A matter of mathematics. A woman with her head in her hands on a park bench. A bird fluttering in an empty gymnasium. The wet, awkward foal attempting to walk. A transfer truck driving by. The stars at noon.

The poem is no match for the feel of human breath on your neck. Waking up with a boner and not being able to remember your dream. An approximation. A rendering. The right lie. Memory. A naked woman drinking a glass of milk in the dark. A strip of negatives in an envelope. The exoskeleton of an image. Words, to trick us. A child's game. We make up the rules as we go along. I burn the you out to get the poem right. A photo is worth 1,000 words. One word is your name.

iii. Dreams

There is an anchor, rising. Some kind of flood has happened. The anchor is floating like a fist. The anchor reminds me of a tattoo on a man's arm which takes the shape of the man's skin as he grows older. A song is coming from somewhere I can't see. The anchor is slowly disappearing in the sky like that red balloon the boy loses in that black-and-white movie. The higher the anchor rises, the further I sink. My wings are drenched. The harder I try to fly, the harder it is to keep my head above water. Finally I take a weird faith in the anchor and let myself fall. The water surrounds me as if it's been waiting for my form to fall through it. It's not fear but something else I feel as some dark thing comes towards me from below.

This, of course, is not the poet's dream at all but the dream of his uncle. But you can't blame the poet; he truly believes it is his dream. He was too young to remember his uncle telling it to him in the valley of the Grand Canyon. It is the dream he knows best, being that it is not his. It grows like a forest in his heart. He is heavy with it, a crucified swimmer. What the poet doesn't know is his uncle still keeps the dream like a faded photograph of a daughter he never had. That once his uncle fell into the well and gave way to the water, he realized his body was heavier than his dream and from then on learned to love the weight that made him drown.

I am walking without moving, a canoe without a body of water. An uncontrollable zoom-in on my hands. Gigantic, heaving. I'm unable to move them, antique radiators attached to my wrists. They swell as if something is trying to get out, but there is no life inside, just dark matter and the remnants of stars. This weight is an anchor holding me to a world which flows all around me like a photograph of electricity. Everything beyond my hands is blotted out and shrinking. Black clouds, un-thunder. I try to free myself from my hands but can't control them; I give up and weather whatever the world will hurl…and with that, the shitstorm begins.

The presence of water is no accident, and even though it only appears once, one gets the feeling it is omnipresent. The canoe is of the Native American variety and is in sharp contrast to the anchor-like feeling of the enormous hands. The dream is a bridge between disappointment and the fear of disappointment—meaning only that the dream will be extended. It's significant that when the dreamer's father comes into the room to calm and comfort the terrified boy, he never mentions he has had the same dream, countless times. It is impossible for the dreamer to forget what he read in a letter once, was it Lowell or his uncle who said, *In Hell, people have huge hands.*

It occurs to me that I need to scream, that perhaps I haven't shouted since I was a child, I mean a full-throated yell to remind me I'm alive, the way a coyote howls or a crow perches on a fence cawing its heart out without any consideration of whether anyone hears or not. But I can't shout like this here in the city—I need to be in the woods alone. So I take the train as far as it goes, walk into the forest until I come to a spot where the sun shines through a clearing in the pines, and release a long, primal scream, expiring every atom of breath in my lungs. A scream without words or reason, until I can no longer emit sound, and I listen to the echo of my voice as if recognizing it for the first time, and feel a flood break inside me, as if my soul itself had been welled up and pushed aside, somehow denied its basic drive, strangely renewed by a single scream. I return from the forest at dusk, take the train back home, and for the first time notice that the city is crawling with wolves.

If a tree falls in a forest…blah, blah, blah. But what if he already lives in the woods alone? His capacity for pain forms a new city. The question should be, do the trees hear a man falling around them, do they recognize him as their own? Clearly, he's been reading his nieces' fairytales again. Despite popular belief, the crow always cares that its cries are heard. Actually, the city is made of embraceable wolves, but how do you expect him to say that? On the train the other day, he saw that someone scribbled on a Vitamin Water poster *your life is what you notice*. A city, a train, a tree, a man. Things fall. Some things never make a sound, but the dreamer hears them all.

I am sitting in a white wicker chair in the middle of a long field. The wind is blowing. The stitching in the chair is coming apart in the seat, creating a sinking sensation. The snake grass comes up to my waist like I was being baptized. A crow is cawing its head off over a lack of seeds or eyes to eat. Although I'm no scarecrow, I realize that I'm tied to the chair. I hear the wind pick up from the west and what sounds like whistling, a familiar tune. In the distance, I can make out what looks like the shape of a cross, but my hair keeps getting in my eyes. The crow has stopped cawing. There is a silence I recognize—the work of a scythe and the stalks of grass against me. Suddenly the field is full of light, and I know a woman is coming to cut my hair.

The dreamer has obviously made some horrible mistake.

I am alone in the audience at a play based on my friend Chris's life. The set is without walls, just a huge mouth opening into a forest. Silence interrupted by the rising sound of panting. Chris, a scrawny whiteboy, comes running from stage left, chased by a group of black boys who want to tie him to a horse and peel his skin off like a tangerine. If captured, he will become their property, perhaps used as a lamp or a farming device. The cloud of boys disappears into the forest and Chris can be heard screaming in the midst of some sort of inquisition. His silhouette stretches out like a giant as he scampers off stage. A set change evokes a long passage of time and Chris's physical transformation into adulthood. Uneasy in his human-skin, he has an unreasonable ache to go back to that place. Trying to disguise himself, he makes a costume out of tree bark and branches and heads back home. He roots himself on a hill in North Carolina. Families sit under him and have picnics in the shade he casts, children climb in his branches, teenagers carve their names into his costume, and nobody ever knows he is not a tree. In spring, to his surprise, his body breaks out in tiny pink and blue flowers. The play ends with the silhouette of a tree in the last seconds of sunlight walking away into the dark night. I can't remember if the curtain falls.

Thinking it was poetry, he once picked up a book called *The Job of Skin*, which turned out to be a Human Genetics dissertation. The thesis statement read: *Skin, at its most primary function, serves as a form of protection.* The labor of being born. Of being black. Color of night. Color of all colors. According to the book, *Skin keeps everything together.* The Collected Books of Myself. The Job of Being White. The Job of Being Chris(t). The Job of Light. The Job of Weight. Identity, blood, race. In North Carolina, all rivers are red. Guilt, a river that runs from Pittsboro to the sea. He once heard a little girl say to no one in particular, "there are trees in the trees." Which evokes what his friend Chris wrote *Wide tree, what are you like?* which due to several learning disabilities he read as *Wide tree, let me in.* The dream can be seen as a third text between the writer and the reader. As opposed to the tree costume, what blossoms is bound to die. *Any skin you see is already dead.* There is a curtain always falling on the dress rehearsals of his forgiveness.

I must be on a boat out in the ocean. I can tell by the flux of birds that follow me like a photographed halo. I can see the markings on their backs, the territories and flags of surrender inside their feathers, each speck in their eyes, a shard of light shimmering on its glass island. Their flight, soundless, infected by some new technology, synchronized, moving together like an accordion, towards some unpronounced existence, flying without any human needs, except to be close to one another, held together by a thin, invisible string, otherwise known as a name.

The Godfather trilogy taught him the importance of family. An inheritance of migration. His sense of morality was a product of *Star Wars*. "What would Luke Skywalker do?" he would ask. In other words, the dream is a warning. When he was 15, he threw a party while his parents were in Hawaii. It grew quickly out of control like a California wildfire. The Gnann brothers broke into his mother's freezer and found the bright-colored bird she'd discovered dead in the forest. They took the frozen bird from the Ziploc bag and played volleyball with it in the kitchen until its head snapped off. Holding the broken bird in his hand, staring at the black wingback, he saw a translucent green appear then disappear, and felt in that instant, the future. Basically he'd always be a big pussy.

The sky is way too blue like a TV set after kids have fucked with the remote, and for a second I don't even see it—an enormous hot-air balloon hovering like the perfect ending to a simile. Then it hits me—this is the bright-striped balloon from the chemistry book I've been editing. I'm driving as if the sky won the war and there are no more roads. Just drifting toward whatever the air offers up. Following the law of we-all-need-a-balloon-to-help-us-home. Hypnotized by the bright balloon and its exquisite interruption of blue, I barely saw them, had to slam my brakes to avoid hitting the four giant buzzards sitting in the middle of the road, their backs to me, congregating over the carcass of something I couldn't see but knew had to be the air from that beautiful balloon.

Impossibly this is an attempt at escape. Gravity, his uncle once told him, is only in your mind. There is a scene from *Before Night Falls* where the dream of escape is so beautiful it outweighs any consequence of the real: one would rather drown going down in a hot-air balloon in the ocean on the way to Florida than remain alive another second without freedom. The dream of it. A carcass of air. Language is secondary to silence. The most beautiful things we do, we do without words. Once, when he was the King of the Forest, he was chased by his brother, Emperor of Grasshoppers, into an overgrown greenhouse, a good 15 feet down the narrow aisle he realized his brother was no longer behind him and alone with the sound of his own breathing, he turned to see he was surrounded by over a dozen giant buzzards roosting eyelevel on marble slabs—the next 10 seconds of this story is the stuff that dreams are made of.

Chased by a guy nicknamed The Moose from my high school gym class, I duck into a dressing room where I hear the soft muzak of the Eurythmics' *Sweet Dreams* and suddenly feel half an urge to dance and half an urge to commit a felony. When I come out, The Moose is gone. I'm looking for a present for my newborn niece. I'm on the third floor and have to get down to the first. But there's only one escalator and it's broken because some child's hand got caught in the part where the rubber goes into the dark heart of the machine. I'm running now because I sense my niece getting older. Finally, I find another escalator, but at the bottom is a body of turbulent water. I'm freaking out because now I have another niece and I have to buy her a present too. Only when I stare at the stairs disappearing into the waves do I realize I have no reason to be worried — I'm an awesome swimmer.

The old "boy-caught-in-the-escalator-story" comes from his grandfather who worked as the sole maintenance man at Sears for 43 years. His grandfather was a master, inside and out, of machines and negative capability. The Moose was actually a girl who tried out for the high school football team, and who the whole school made fun of. Alone, he felt sorry for her and wanted to talk to her but picked on her in public so his friends would think he was cool. Once, when they were both waiting in the principal's office and no one was around, she plucked a June bug out of his oily hair and when she went to open her hand to show him, it burst into the air, spread its wings and in a flash of green and gold, flew across the room and out the door. His niece is now six-feet tall.

All around town, through sound-bites, overheard conversations and subway chatter, on the cover of magazines, in various clips on every TV in every window, the news came like a kind of second weather—inexplicably, Joba Chamberlain had lost his pinpoint control, his stats were plummeting downward, his E.R.A was ballooning, he was plunking batters left and right, he kept blowing saves and the Yankees kept losing. And somehow it was all my fault, and all of New York hated me. Chased down the streets, I quickly ducked into a dark alley to avoid getting murdered by the citizens of New York City, amassing into an angry mob. Shrouded in this fear, it occurred to me that I contained multitudes, that I too was a cloud, a black storm of some unknown gathering order, a swarm, a halo of black gnats hatching and re-hatching in the hair and eyes of the living, predestined to haunt and continually exhume, and that somewhere, another army of winged things would also find me and descend when the moment arrived, that I'd have to reach back for an arrow of pure clean fire in order to save all these souls coming to crucify me, even if I'll never know why.

There is a certain horror in the materialization of a dream that is unlike anything else a person can endure. Of course, the dreamer *is* Joba Chamberlain. He *is* the people of New York, the hate and fear, the multitudes, the saved and the savior, the bearer and the weight. He is all creation, clouds, insects, and the elements, since energy is never lost, only changes shape like the fire he'll reach back for, always forthcoming, forever and arrow, amen. He is afraid of losing his "mojo," being drained of magic, suffering under the "curse" of finishing anything (also known as "the Bambino"), since for the dreamer, finishing is a defeat, a kind of death. It is necessary for the dream to remain just-in-the-distance, serving its role, its job, proverbial water on a stick. The real horror comes from knowing his dreams will end when he loses the language to describe them.

I am carrying a weight like an anvil or wooden cross. It is either far too quiet or the birds are way too loud, as if a sound technician turned off the world in order to isolate the noise of the birds to prove their existence. In my lap is a bright white manuscript. There are no words on the first page, just a whiteness without end. I place the manuscript down with an unspoken hope like a bowl of milk set out for a missing cat. A page rises up into the yard like a white flag into the green, green grass. Imagine inventing snow. As the last page tumbleweeds away, I can make out black markings and immediately recognize them as that of a foreign language. Inexplicably, I know exactly how to pronounce each word, even though the shapes and letters are strange, and as they leave me, I know they are frightening and beautiful and all my name.

Metaphors are butterflies. And vice versa. The dreaded dream of being awake. The weight the dreamer carries is "wait." A symptom of his dyslexia. A wait not of arrivals, but of returns. An uncle, a manuscript, a name. And the winds that carry them into the universe, a voice awaiting its unrecognized echo. The manuscript (like the recording of birds) is not proof of his existence, rather it is his existence. Born waiting. What the dreamer walks toward. A door, standing before us, beaming in whiteness, in the place of all we know. Real butterflies.

I'm underwater again. Above me a family of gray whales pass, weightless as clouds. They are so light they seem to slowly slip away like a fist full of balloons. In their presence I feel my own weight withdraw, sunward. They emit a sound which travels through my body like light through blue water. It is a sound of longing so strong I know a flock of birds live inside the whales, calling out to each other in the dark not to lose one another. As the family of whales disappears into the distance, the sound they made has turned into a voiceover of a man and I'm not underwater at all, but inside a TV show about whales. Suddenly conscious that I'm a corporeal being, complete with lungs and common phobias, I sink. I flail my arms and inhale mouthfuls of seawater. As I choke and drown, I see gray whales descending upon me as they open their jaws to swallow me, a thick stream of birds bursts from their mouths and gathering and bustling beneath me like a wave, raise me up through the surface, as if the sea didn't want me, until I am suspended in a purgatory between the sky and the sea.

If you pay attention, you'll see that water appears then disappears. The birds, being birds, are allowed, whether living inside of whales or televisions, to fly around in there bewildered by the sea's blue, without any thought of water, without any thought of… "Blubber is blubber, you know," Melville says in a letter where he pretends not to be drowning. *What good does it do to caress an ocean?* is the only sentence he remembers from the hundreds of lost letters his uncle wrote him right before he died. If the caress is wasted, better then, that in his love for the ocean, he throw his entire body into the water and swim blindly as long as allowed. Perhaps the ocean still would not understand such pure intentions, but wait for him to drown, something that might be the corresponding expression of the ocean's love, of which he couldn't possibly endure, being a man. Perhaps.

There is simply color. A chromatic block containing the property of being able to be walked into, and which appears to have no end. I enter this new primary which rapidly dissolves, like a crayon in the sun, into a mutation of the relationship between colors, or the lack of one. All the colors bleed into the same significance, a toneless, mute whiteness like a star in the sunlight, and as if falling, suddenly accelerates into a sound. Now there is only sound, I won't say music, since that would be a lie. There is simply sound with no beginning and no end. A sound so strong I can no longer hear anything, just a sensation of space. An endless space in which black and white become a bed to tumble in like Dorothy in *The Wizard of Oz*. The sound holds me up like the memory of leg wrestling a loved one, it's not exactly floating, but whatever it is, I know it will end…*it never ends.*

The dreamer lost the painter's hat his uncle gave him right before he drowned. The dream is an attempt at peace in the face of the fact that anyone has to die. The dream is just a dream. He was told he'd go blind if he stared at the sun too long. That was 32 years ago. It's been said that the problem with peace is boredom. I say shut up and close your eyes.

iv. The End of the Sea

The boy, mostly seaweed, was born in the forest. Specifically, where the forest meets the sea—a floor of dead things and trees that won't budge to any music, that complain about their roots, that don't know if they are dead or not, that listen to the boy's thoughts like a radio, occasionally swaying to his anger or leaked dreams, but mostly that compose a darkness, a darkness that is its own color, a darkness that opens up into a bright shoreless sea. The sea where everything, eventually, ends.

He knew the sea was not the sea. That the real sea was hidden. A forest. From the air his body became a da Vinci drawing drowning in ink. Underwater, everything had the feeling of felt, the inside of music. Even as he floats, he's aware the forest is there, a living shadow, a place to pass through to what he imagines is home. Secrets entwined as seaweed. Reaching the shore, he stares at the water, as if waiting for something, anything, to rise.

His mother was blind and his father's right leg did not fit his left leg. His little sister swore he was a superhero who could fly through glass. Afraid, he moved further and further from home until all he remembered was the darkness and the smell of the sea. He wrote books in the dark. He wrote a book called *King of the Forest* about a boy born in the forest, whose mother was blind and whose father had a hollow leg. A book of howling. A book that only the creatures of that kingdom could understand. He wrote like he was diving into the ocean to see if the sea ever ends.

The boy was just a boy, the seaweed was hair, the forest, a stand of North Carolina pines, and the sea was a man-made lake where he got a rusty hook stuck in his foot and made castles out of catfish bones. The forest was a place to get lost in when his parents were fighting. A place to walk, a walk that always ends at the edge of water. A collection of stars, broken glass, and other dead things. His mother has excellent vision, his father was a tennis player, and his sister tried to stab him for stealing her big red ball. He worshiped his uncle. Of course, he disappeared, like all things do. The boy grew up. He loved and longed and disappointed and was constantly forgiven. It is a sad story. He wrote a book about it. Called it *King of the Forest*.

Sampson
Starkweather

LA

LA

LA

SAMPSON STARKWEATHER

did you say river
without *bend*
or *end*
if it didn't hurt
I'd have gone
a long time ago
good looking
out Pain
everything is a game
the pesky not-world
hiding somewhere
I want poems
to be like 80s video games
land and sky
forever off
either side of the screen
New Zealand is like that
two horizons
that never come
together
are you wet yet
you love when I talk
landscape in overalls
scamper the flattened world
pick up
the occasional coin
or sledge hammer
someday
I'll mushroom-leap
those goddamn digital clouds
we lie
under
and cry

in the end
Hamlet was a zombie piece
it doesn't take
a souped-up ambulance
to catch ghosts
or metaghosts
we rest on
the shoulders of electricians
imagine how the phone feels
when it rings
we talked so long
I fell asleep in that position
sorta seahorse
floating back
through the threshold
of the other side
of the sky
why can't I get closer
to rainbows
multiple choice tests
offer possible answers
churches are more specific
now-a-days
did you say riots
are passé or blasé
gimme one good mantra
not rooted in baby talk
power of attorney is power of attorney
is what I always say
history is that kid
who transferred in the 9th grade
with a tape recorder
duct-taped to his chest
like a bomb
like a friend
he was writing a book
whatever happened to him
happened

email me an animal
that doesn't die
leaving a stinger
inside something without
a simile like
I'm pretty
sure the things
that kill you
make you
stronger too
so what
the word
word is in sword
tell me something
useful like how
I will die
so I can die
in another way
I'm trying
to make breathing
more like dancing
sleep is melodramatic
as if anyone could be
that calm
come on
sell me something
everything must go
is another way to say
nothing can stay
pure emptiness
is a pipe-dream
angsty teenagers
skateboard in
this close
to a new kind
of nothing
like the nothing
between nothing
my life
passes through

let the fish go
there is a limit
to all things
except the way light gathers
on the ground
around a certain circle of trees
I have dubbed thee
knights of qua
because of the way you kiss
I've reconsidered
this breathing thing
the sun is a terrorist
your skin pretends
to protect the soft parts
that lie inside
did you see the sign
about the fish
there was nothing I could do
to stop the bleeding
I took the hook out
the way you taught me
the more animal
the less pain
something rising
inside the light
stupid shadow
human is the state of the wound
stagger to the edge
of the woods
suck the poison out
watch me
hide from the sun
with this rainbow snow cone
lost and found
in the pines
in the pines

light is awesome!
there should be a mind Olympics
imagine my mug
on a Wheaties box
a golden metaphor
which is where
every metaphor should stop
I can do anything
with money
I'll show you
if you give me the money
I too believe
in rivers
over slogans
define *employed*
I'm working
on carving
through the earth
my desire-map
is running
out of room
like that guy who grew
a garden of knives
to combat a lack of silver
in nature
there is a name for death
by sadness
but forget it
a cracked lcd screen
uninsured
and damn good at it
I write
to become
historically
alone

love is so competitive
we're all losers
I understand
those kids
who hide
in abandoned refrigerators
cultivating a quiet
hum
mmmmmmmmmmmm
looks like birds
escaping the page
my life feels
like a dove
in the hands
of an amateur magician
I'm entering
your last sentence
in a beauty contest
everyone knows
reading is the realist
shit ever
see we will
all die
of an imperceptible sadness
can't you reproduce
any faster
nothing's private
about our parts
or our wholes
beyond space
I am a star
in the movie trailer
for the end
of the world

that Microsoft course
saved my life
the first time
we fucked
I thought I was an astronaut
forgot to breathe
did it happen
if it didn't feel real
the novelization
of this poem
would require words
to become vampires
which means
it will be nothing
like what it is like
to be trapped inside
these broken view-finders
we call bodies
wouldn't be a bad job
if you didn't have
to pay it all back
I keep all my friends
on a spreadsheet
in case I miss them
just once I'd like
to breastfeed
hard to believe
you are still listening
to this horribly
translated joke
where are the
track changes
for this life
no rescue
sea of red

syntactical revolution
is real
language is going
to get up
and bust
some heads
ever feel
like a gang
of exclamation points
is following you
boo
holes appear whole
night is just a map
of night
disappearing
at all times
the sun shines
Texas is this crazy
fucker's dream
someone forgot
to turn off
it gets good
at the 3:33 mark
where static meets the sky
clouds crumble
I wish I was
as resilient
as email
a dictionary of sighs
not a single dream
since the surgery
gravity is a pretty
boring story
up to
the part
where I
defy
defy
defy

the first step
is to cake yourself
in self-identity cream
look at these trees
pretending to be
trees
nature is a real nuisance
try putting the black back
in a bird
I am full
of ineffective action
what does it mean
if you shit
in a dream
there is a tear
in your consciousness
a rip in the shape
of me running
international icon
for everything
about to burn
even oceans
pawn oars
we are the easiest animal
to hunt
permanent season
of elegy
here comes
a thousand doves
apparently we
need love
coo

when in large groups
I often want to swing
Thor's hammer
I call it POWER POETRY
transforming irritability
into energy
should win a prize
for almost existing
like a superlove
how weird is becoming
a tunnel
more of a pastime
than an act
of civil engineering
no gland
to regulate this emotion
life is another way to say
proportional to
the push-button moment
take *Escape* from every
keyboard
I am the goat
perched on anything
a branch of shame
the denial
that one is one's own
flag
things don't have
to be
whole
to break
everything
is an action
watch the poem
sail into
itself

imagine this as music
dunzo
now where to go
there is light
then there isn't
no one mentions
the shadow massacre
every night
I promise
women who put their heads
in those space helmets
are holy
if you review the tape
technically I fell in love
with your purse first
remember that play I wrote
with naked people
crouched in trees
screaming SHUT UP CROW
as human-sized birds sit poolside
the critics all cried
I don't know why
I get so romantic
night is pretty
normal
words make us do dumb things
why does everyone assume
I'm watching the Super Bowl
speaking of light
step right in
to a field
party in Pittsboro
poke the fallen
for signs of life
nothing still
maybe a wave
from this distance
there is no way to say
it wasn't beautiful

the trick is to transcend
your to-do list
who couldn't use
some more *la la la's*
in their life
I live mine
masturbatorily
to what degree
are we citizens
of the argument
whether everything
suddenly wants
to live or love or does
it matter
an ongoing battle
between belief
and these wildfires
like a poem
writing itself
genius is just a feeling
of being
very uncertain
everything is more beautiful
out of context
my religion is searching
for a real moment
of text
which will blow away
I know this wind
from somewhere
it came
bearing
I almost said
flowers

lop off your obligatory birds
pretty ain't an alibi
bambi was asking for it
tv taught me
happiness is not having
poison ivy
werewolves are sexy
true tragedy
is all your friends
getting high
without you
the lack of hot people
on this train
is alarming
there must be some cord
to pull
this here
is known
as the kindle-fist-bump
ever feel like a bobble-head
without a head
the lifespan
of a snowman
elephant grass
and a push-mower heart
still tinkering
with the sticky-bomb poem
perfect for tight quarters
or parties ripe
with white people
music over the balcony
the slow fall of money
pretending
to be green snow
makes me jealous
begging for some
new kind of storm
bend me over
whisper something
no one's ever said
before

to seek a simple
something that loves
itself
doesn't have to mean
masturbation y'all
lie down
I'll show you
my press
yes
when we pull apart
shazam
customized shipwrecks
down to the smallest detail
you can't get
jellyfish to float
like this
don't lick
the igloo
kids keep clear
of scuba gear
brass tax
how much
for your island
your gorgeous sunburn
what if I'm already
under water
all the time
this is love
or reverse placebo effect
a billboard dedicated
to the way you talk
if you love me
unlock your phone
see those two lights
on the sea
that's me
that's me
that's me

more than poetry
the mechanical turtles
of Chinatown leave
their mark
too green
to believe
there's no opposite for
the real
truth lies
the wrung-sponge
where speech comes from
creates a motor
the world turns
from my anger
it's a joy
one can't invent
the idea
of invention
an act of the ego
to say
I did that
edifice of air
how I got lost
on a field trip
to the planetarium
the scars still shine
people point
name names
the million misfires
of shame
the Jewish girl's birthday
on a battleship
must've been beautiful
young things
dancing on the
poop deck

I dug your horror-movie intro
feathers everywhere
still how calm was that guy
on Oprah
just thinking about the world
will turn anyone
into Rick James
I thought it was an actual statue
of limitations
imagine the pigeon shit
ever call in a bomb threat
on your crying baby
I feel like doing that
all the time
lead by a lack of dreams
every suit is the wrong suit
I can do anything
voila a cupcake
going up in flame
never-ending
amateur night
it doesn't take much
to amaze
these minions inside
my computer
I've been talking to children
about whether
bee shit exists
it's difficult
pretending to be snow
there are so many things
to cover
just being yourself
the dove
the crow
the dove

every poem should begin
I'm kind of in a dunebuggy
it's a fact
feelings of powerlessness
lead to killing and shopping
sprees weeeeeeee
a growing demand
for designer vaginas
in other news
ghost slugs are real
people can be so quiet
they barely exist
images of earth
always make me horny
it sounds
like a soap opera
when it hums
all God's children
are brats
products of
product placement
know when to say when
how dumb is that
just keep going
swallow sand
try to finalize
any love
endless
like the games
people play
on the subway
get in
follow me
anywhere

direction is arbitrary
when driving through a desert
blankets of snow
make no sense
when you said
I felt like a documentary
on darkness my heart began
to implode
lord don't let me be haunted
by poor directions
to a party in Brooklyn
with the woman I love
sure there's a market for it
I'm telling you
the squirrels are up to something
just ask the trees
growing up
with progressive parents
is like a trailer for an SNL movie
where they show all the good parts
you spend a bunch of money
and time for nothing
a fortune
teller told me the loss
of video tape will destroy me
memory's reprise
it's getting cold outside
I'm not speaking figuratively
apparently throwing up the horns
doesn't translate in this country
why is it always Ezra Pound with you
a computer has learned
to identify beauty
it's likely the sky
is upside down
people are starving
wake me up
when we reach
the giant peach

here's the deal
there are 3 kinds
of actual sadness
which will not be
addressed here
for reasons of decency
this is what happens
when the wind
gets bored
at parties
I put my brain
on shuffle
my thoughts
are like Baldwin brothers
tangled in a heated game
of Twister
under job description
I put CEO of Alone
guilt is a just feeling
you have
when you are alive
we all need a sky
to fall through
or body of water
something blue
end without end
I always thought
a rockless place
was impossible
how will we know
we've hit bottom
without it
but now I know
it's the secret
we all share

I saw a man siphoning gas
it looked like he was praying
someone should probably follow
up on that
I'm often cramming
for a driving test
in my dreams
questions consume me
I read a book about the history
of radiators
and decided I loved you
it felt like money thrown
into a public fountain
with a cherub peeing
someone keeps leaving
these pamphlets on abstinence
under my windshield
the future
a role-playing game
a flip book
of a man falling
you're going to have
to install something
if you want to read
the rest
dance with the surplus
in late iPhone light
parking is at the heart
of every decision
and indecision
birds are so meta
even their chirps
describe themselves
blame it on the sky
now point to it
lightning
stick around this time

shoulder blades should
replace knives
beauty get a grip
I don't understand
why stars don't
look up to us
who remembers
being born
in the 70s
it was draining
being a democrat
premature dreams
girls still make me feel
like styrofoam planets
in the solar system I made
for the 4th grade science fair
thermodynamics are whack
I won't be leaving my house
for a while
I wish I could be a part
of some party
what I really wish
is to be alone
without feeling alone
to make sense
of these lines
I want to go home
find you
have been living
beneath my bed
take off
our clothes
lie back
and talk and talk
until it's ruined
the stars

please accept my eggs
Sallie Mae
one installment away
from posthumously
being in the black
the brain contains
a neuron to identify
Jennifer Aniston
hope is pretty
perverted
people prefer cars
that look angry
all's fair in war
and whatever
as far as gerunds go
bleeding is better
than annoying
some astronaut said
space smells
like hot metal   .
and fried steak
there's no
up or down
when you're in the dark
fur is frightening
the bird inside
the egg
the egg inside
the bird
disappointed
with the world
chirp chirp
you're all dead

the key to anger
is direction
and government funding
what was it
you said
a kind of headless
guilt emerges
when will some bodiless
peace descend
what a weather
we're having
I think I'll climb a tree
an apathy tree
so this is where you've been
hiding the apology
is it wrong
I want to 69
your thoughts
reason has always worked
this way
a storm drain
in my rib cage
collecting no
new knowledge
how the hurt comes
headless as a star
you can see inside of
where music goes
don't turn around
don't be fooled
by this voice
there's no
switch to throw
for this sort of thing

wanna see
my dead swan
the best pick-up lines
involve chloroform
just your staple
circus story
ending in an ellipsis
the world's last sentence
waving
a torn flag
like a plot summary
reverse apocalypse
radio crackle
is my favorite song
says here under occupations
conquistador of everything
why won't my plants die
the cop told me
buy low sell high
maybe I'm a martyr
praying to an accident
electricity and your hamstring
are things I'd like
to lick
the heart beats
a savage
aristocrat in its cube
how can you know so much
about my silence
my nightmares
my dream job
would be
sunlight

shape up clouds
one of these days
people are bound
to look up
be amazed
to classify
butterflies and moths
remember their lives
in the cocoon
we too will come out
of some forest to see
a marooned submarine
what are these leagues
under the sea
how do I become one
corrections facility
has a great ring to it
don't you think
we're all pretending
to be brave
or afraid
in other words
the mask
of a Mexican wrestler
give up
language
Up Up
Down Down
Left Right
Left Right
A B Select Start
these stupid clouds
won't move
by themselves
it's exhausting
trying
to stop time

have you noticed pussyfoot
is always singular
iron-lung killjoy
sound like bad ass Indians
take the longest breath
anyone's ever taken
and begin again
the poem is its own
audience
scientists say the soul
has the consistency
of an expensive milkshake
bagpipes are bad
for the environment
Dear Mom
you don't know shit
about poetry
if you were a think tank
we'd all be making
cartoon balloons
I love hitting
Undo poof
I made the rain
go away
your name is # 2
on my things to do list
Google Earth knows dick
about my birthmarks
let's all change
color
what are people
who study traffic
called
a lot of love
has died
technically
anything can be
counted

skin is the shit
dying and being born
at the same time
detritus isn't
a video game
let's trace
the shape of the universe
goose bumps sunburn
open sky
a city of fields
if light bends
why can't we
become a curve
a visible equation
I have love
like a headache
sure you can cut a hole
in a sheet
but good luck
trying to fuck a ghost
hello plasma
it's me
fellow fake
state of matter
born with a parachute
I can't stop
hovering
help me holes
hold me or enlighten
the secret of life
is being tan
give me your wallet
did you think
this poem
was going to end
by itself

remember when wind
was invented
those were the days
a future
without waiting
love is shaky
at Best Buy
a bobble head doll
of allah
would just be
a floating body
I'd say the maker
went overboard
with these stars
silence
is so money
you hear me
breathing machine
so long
little levee
something escapes
my love
is historic
google me
I'm a serial killer
the past
never leaves
ask the skeleton
from the 7th grade
it still whistles
it still bleeds
hey wind
why don't you
blow me

yay vacation
in the ruins
watch what happens
when you doubt
me you'll see
I'm a black belt
in pussying-out
so sorry
about your
fourth wall
I needed something
to chop
I'm 33 and still
don't understand the birds
and the bees
seriously do they fuck
or what
am I the only one
who thinks
we might be the brainchild
of some sad omnipotent man's
dream for a theme park
everything gets dark
technically it's
eggplant rain
I'd love to partake
but I've got
umbrellas and promises
to break
and miles to go
before this roofie wears off
and miles to go
before this roofie wears off

sitting backward
on the train
is like time-traveling
light a candle
when someone dies
a match
when we shit
poetry
is the kid who keeps
asking why
until there are
no more answers
except the cold
outside not
to mention in
we are trembling
that's all you got sun
now hand me some
crayons and stand
back it's Halloween
in my head
the leaves drop
around me
like a disease
it's a travesty
the moon
hasn't been
Employee of the Month
at least once
I get to make
the rules mom
absolutely
no dying

mystery is predictable
zodiacal bullshit
loneliness empties
its bullets
if I become
possessed
at least let me speak
some crazy-ass Latin
I used to think
school spirit
meant my high school
had a ghost
what's the weather
when you're drowning
basically blue
an MFA
in shipwrecks
extract salt and fear
and the sea
wouldn't be
a bad place
to be employed
a pension in
swimming lessons
tell me how
not to be me
I am speaking
from the heart
remote
barless
ready to beat
you
to death

the army should do something
about these poetry readings
feel free
to read this
left to right
if it helps
I'll remove
the gimp mask
I was going
for an aura thing
put on
the wrestling
I wanna become
more human
gonna make
for great television
Pimp my Poem
totally cancelled
after no seasons
I've been emailing
people I forget
are dead again
how big is the wind
anyway there's no
way to prove
love exists
unless you believe
the glittered script
of my 8th grade
t-shirt
YES WAY!

this is not magic
yet 2.3 frat boys
die every year
pouring alcohol
in their ass
a wooden rabbit
watches you
it feels weird
to be at the mercy
of so much
after I die
I hope
someone comes
out with my Selected
Early and Awesome Poems
what were dreams
like before movies
besides boring
and seriously lacking
special effects
for art's sake
there must be a way
to get police
dogs to leap
out of the screen
I agree
breatharianism is a crock
but how cool would it be
to shit sunlight
god should give me
a grant for this
all I'm asking
is to own
a building
so people have
to call me
super

how do mountains happen
I say Windows 98
and the world begins
to weep
wish my restless leg
would spread
to the rest
of me
please don't bleed
on the free
upholstery
I'm not a poet
I just crush a lot
ever think the god
that put us here
forgot to punch
holes in the jar
ouroboros of the inside
how dare you
come gradual
like a landscape
or appreciation
of art
no question
coyotes have the coolest
dynamite
neither empirically
good or bad
but beautiful still
see
I came
all over
the mountain

need a cheat code
for Mondays
a way to TiVo
the times
I've been brave
a find-and-replace
for my face
I've learned a lot
from a man
in a doughnut suit
made a decent living
misunderstanding
my name
technically
it's "spree killer"
watch me work
grass are you getting
this down
we don't know jack
about the ground
good luck
with your MFA
in cut-n-paste
health care
is killing me
drowning
in a sea
of mediocrity
luckily I was born
with these
sweet ass
water-wings

fuck god
I made a pond once
in the small
of your back
from the air
it's often mistaken
for Los Angeles
or a polar bear
exhibit déjà vu
is no joke
this life is on
a loop I swear
I see you everywhere
just breathing
like that
your witchcraft is whack
this quiz
will tell you
who you are
and why
you're here
time to harvest
the pain-farm friends
the problem with being
in love
is there is nothing
to think about
language is as real
as it gets
groceries feel good
take that
however you want
the question should be
does god believe
in us

who knew
something so broken
could keep breaking
is it impetus
or impotence
of dreams
see I'm a star
collapsing
a new degree
of black
I think I left
the burner on
I admit it
I died
and still sold nothing
I'm accruing a weapons cache
so I can constantly refer
to my weapons cache
we all must shoo
the big black birds
of our psyche
O big train
I'm gonna kiss
your face
this place is crawling
with babies
did we do that
I'm sorry for leaving
my glitter inside you
you call these drugs
no wonder
nothing works
the goddamned cloud machine
is jammed again
at the end
of this poem
someone is going
to die
just you wait

similes suck
nothing is like
something else
see what I mean
black and white is boring
until you realize
they're every color
all at once
I'm bending time
into a boomerang
and aiming for your face
I'm not violent
but I'm going to kill
these crows
for being so crow-y
why can't nature
be out of its nature
for once
I'd like to disappear
in some glory-hole of snow
melt everything
I enter everything
I touch
a snowman
in reverse
feel free
to drink from me
I agree
shadows are distracting
but from what
someday we'll bloom
into a sentence
so simple
it will seem like a mistake
the world is grey
so what are you
waiting for
go crow
and fuck a dove

caucasian magic
is another way
to say politics
this shit's gonna get me
rich
earthlings you dance
dorky
you're not going
to haunt
ghosts in those
overalls are you
awesome
because I am
sitting in the so-called
silence
a philanthropist
of birds
listening to that
awful racquet
as kids explicate
the ridiculous
rules and names
of marble games
I love fisting life
a character
wandering
out of a story
waiting for some
freaky phenomena
to happen
something
must fall
from the sky
if that giant
keeps shaking the shit
out of it
once upon a time
the end

clusterfucks
aren't a breakfast cereal
but I start my day
that way
a man ate an entire car
a Buick I believe
which pretty much
sums up the species
the whole world
smells like semen
or is it just me
sometimes I pretend
my penis is a paint brush
and you know
we make art
I'm telling you
the clouds point
to us too
make up names
for the shapes we take
how do we live
answer me that
Web MD
this is going
nowhere
I should just dance
my face off
for the next 20 seconds
that would be weird
good weird
like if it rained
old baseball cards
or mixed tapes
by shy kids in love
with girls way out
of their league
play 'em
'til the tapes break

war would be cooler
if they had bone zones
instead of kill zones
kiss me
been handling
money
& life devices
wouldn't it
be worse
to be a standing
duck
now that there's
a yoga position
slaying since 1861
the not-so-civil war
blood on the keyboard
spiritual pop ups
dizzy by
bright lipstick
2 of my machines
have fallen in love
I'd like to thank
the sewing team
for The Heart is Green
why do I have all this
foreign money
which one of you
is the real fake Michael Jackson
nothing ever
feels new
O cable guy
my cable guy
how much
to hook up
some transcendence
or at least
some HBO

congratulations
your podcast ruined
our dance party
I'd breathe
but it's been done before
wanna invent
some new shit
to do
with oxygen
scientists say
the earth sounds
like a refrigerator
I hope the soldiers
never leave
this town
the flame-thrower guy
is really growing
on me
night is a trick donkey
like how do we know
there's not constantly
black lightning striking
or dark constellations
that could tell us
about our personalities
and what mysterious
person is about
to enter
our lives
is there something
other
than a wide berth
people are so into
their kids
but I get it
like how
I made
everyone I know
see this shit
I just took

this forest
is unusually horny
even the tress
speak legalese
ummmm nasty
gonna need a staple-remover
when I'm through
with you
promise I won't
come until you
sneeze
learned it
from a book
now run outside
and play
with your idea
art is for
children
shake me
like a pom-pom
in a little white fist
watch me
stand
for something
with nothing
to say
maybe we should
make out god
don't you
just love
love

responsibility & disappointment
on either side
of my nunchucks
you might want
to stand back
I'm about to break
the 8th wall y'all
yes there will be asbestos
little birds of it
exploding in white dust
like the pigeon
I saw a homeless guy
punch in mid air
no that's not what
hermetically sealed means
if anxiety could save
people you'd be
a superhero
of hanging out
the end
of *Ghostbusters*
would have been better
if the *Stay Puft Marshmallow Man*
was replaced
with John Ashbery's junk
there comes a time
when we all must cross
the streams
think of the nothing
coming
to destroy us
don't turn around
I'm thinking
of it
now

I am small
but make
big music
the silence is so
drop-kickable
if you could look
into my brain
it would look like
the sound of the emergency
broadcast system
as if we didn't all
have an eagle
thrashing in our thorax
it's time
to maim maims
once and for all
I'd like to bludgeon
violence to death
pardon me I didn't see
your sheriff's badge
believe me
I loved you
before roads
alive and in the air
I dreamed I dreamed
a radio melting
the sun
eventually everything falls
apart and resembles
itself
we are always losing
something
but what
we have
finally become

who doesn't desire
to break things
without reason
travel by submarine
then power out
some crunches
had hoped to see a beheading
from bed
but was forced
to get up
clean my rifle
and Skype my wife
the world will end
like this
or a commercial
for the clapper
where an old woman
claps her hands
then the lights
go out
and the plants'
dance party begins
putting the "a" back
in asexual
boredom bores me
why can't we
have it all
in pill-form
make transformer noises
and bloom
into metal bodies
this poem
will not change
your life
unless
it does
hope floats
the way dead
people do
patience comes
from outerspace

the crows know
sorrow comes
to all
one little iguana heart
at a time
tougher than hell
to chew
I watch the Rambo trilogy
before work
religiously
because there is no insurance
for certain situations
this is the part
where a Fiat disappears
into the distance
and a eucalyptus tree
participates in mystery
I invented a new
checkers move
called international-symbol-for-time-
to-tuck-your-penis-
between-your-legs
people want to feel
safe
does the fire
have its own exit sign
for the not-fire
I read on this dude's tattoo
consumerism is natural
so is evil
this is that
but so is this
the ache of the familiar
any dream as text
like the Constitution
on parchment paper
disintegrating when exposed
to human breath
or finding a Post-it
from a girl you loved
telling you to get your

own goddamn sample
of lobster bisque
with impossible patience
like everyone who's ever died
sitting down in a room
would make a shitty
lifetime original movie
or metaphor
life is a river
with throat cancer
what a great place
to make camp
human taxidermy is legal
with the right permits
I'm walking against
the idea
we must die
towards Pittsboro
heading south
looking for anything
green
past black fields
that feel more
like memory
than memory can
kids it turns out
this life is super
fucking hard
love a run-
away sidecar
attached
to no motorcycle
I want to go
where email goes
brave as the tiny birds
stuck inside JFK airport
chirping like a ringtone
afraid of nothing
dump trucks tend to feel
inferior is how
I wanted to start

this letter to you
but wasn't sure
where to go
from there
according to the back
of the box
we all die piecemeal
science is the elimination
of dreams I aim for
the pain within
pain
we are close
there is no mistaking
that bashful elephant
floating above us
or the nightmare where
we're pecked to death
by baby birds
now back up
and watch me
nightstick the shit
out of this piñata
of light

SAMPSON STARKWEATHER

The 77 poems that comprise *The Waters* are transcontemporations of César Vallejo's 1922 masterpiece *Trilce*. A transcontemporation is to a poem what RoboCop is to a normal police officer.

I

Certain haircuts can bring back the dead.
This year I'll wear the ocean, shorn.

A little more Alka Seltzer
to make these seagulls shut up, a little
more net for the things that glean. I hear
they're putting famous swimmers
on stamps. I figured you'd like that.
Anything but birds. *Fear is merely a matter*
of amino acids, you once told me
at the top of the Grand Canyon.

A little more elbow room
in the knee, home movies of ghosts
         BENEATH THE BLUEST WATERFALLS

The day you taught me how to shave
and play dead, you said *hair is what holds the world*
together

II

Torpedo. Torpedo.

Time is another name for what the fuck happened/happens.
Bored in the belly of a battleship, we played Hearts without cards.
Torpedo. Torpedo.

Eros. Eros.

I cut the head off a rooster to see if it really
ran around like everybody said. Night, unable to coagulate.
Eros. Eros.

Manzanita. Manzanita.

The bush burns, before fire, unusual rain.
There is no point to this poem except to slow you down a little.
Manzanita. Manzanita.

Ocean. Ocean.

What's the moon got to do with it?
What's blacker than anything?
Ocean. Ocean.

III

Fuck the flood, this wake
would make a great movie-trailer
for Time and his henchmen. Some story…
always at the edge of its measure.
Select theaters in my head.

She left me with a cupboard full of weird teas,
pistol-whipped by desire and the world's
saddest TV, tuned to suffering or
Charlie Rose—I take to the roof
to watch the moon rocking
        its gold tooth.

Your hurricane name offends me.
That goat we placed our faith in,
perched on the fencepost, is gone.
Heartbreak vs. average rainfall
and gone is another way to say *here*.

The litter of blind things we found drowned
beneath the double-wide told us it would end like this:
we are very tired, we are very very,
we had gone back and forth all night on the very—
how does the dream get more dream?

The Water is Rising
        Pleas

IV

Reagan supplied the Contras condoms:
strawberry, cinnamon, plutonium, and AIDS flavored —
a place to put their children. What did we ever do
to deserve ourselves, private jihads of "more stuff,"
subject to random search based on being born
where you're born. Everything ends with an –ism.

A poll says the Tin Man is Iran's favorite
Wizard of Oz character. The dreams of heart
surgeons should be our #1 export. Entering
and leaving, an existence. Other animals
have mastered how to part, how to not want
mother. How to make mother into hammer. It's
                        the metal.
It's the absence of any search of the unseen.
The distance, best of all,
between the womb and the dirt.

In holy wars, weapons are always archaic —
I see spears and arrows, products of trees, at most
a sword, barbed in what the people want to hear.
Language like lead.

Heat. Ovary. Nearly bird.
Born into burning. Born into hammers.
When Reagan died, he remembered no-
thing. Nothing remembered the rest.

V

Iron Man was how I survived 1989, oxidized,
a suit to protect us. A boy from Phoenix sketching birds
in a foxhole in Vietnam is buried in my memory
like a bookmark of every forgotten. Never under-
stood the urge to kill what could fly, never knew the weight
of iron — no armor for an ocean.

In the basement, I found the comic book
of questions your body became:
#2, the war between minor bones, the hollow
thigh (t)issue, a strand of blond hair
caught in a door hinge, other-
wise known as the "dead hero" era.

Chainmail, Sam(urai) sword, or OP® shorts?
Kiddie pool, quarry, or ocean? Who saves us
from so many hushes and screams, so many waves
of why? Who shakes free the trembling rivers of moths?
Cartoons, iron, words — who protects me
from future-me?

O Iron Man, rusted beyond re⁺
cognition.

VI

Each time you bleed, you come back to me
changed, more trapped-animal than Rilkian
angel, spurious, these seeds blown from the tree
alone in the abdomen where we watch the green sun
go down for fractions of infinity. Want is another game
with rules like water, with an objective to kill
the other's _____, the logos, locked in its kiva
of hate. Another poem without horses, a mild debate
about what animal noises to make, leads
to full-scale sex on the rain-making machine.

Someone could walk on this nebula
of inner fluids migrating in the kitchen, shhhhh,
someone's coming. Stay still and I'll tell you
about the teeth marks on your breasts, the search
for an organ like an eyelid or a valve,
an aqueduct for all this wanting.

God is a hole
in your blue-jeans, this alone is the secret
of his omnipotence. He lives
in Chappaqua, he has souls to save. I want to axe
whoever said, *"These are the days of our lives."*
Truth, the black milk of tomorrow. Quietly, you've stolen
away with my favorite coffee cup. Watching
your car grow smaller, I'm suddenly sad
                        knowing your god
has more arms than mine.

VII

A Rubik's Cube with the stickers peeled off—
the point is—everything is impossible. Cubism was a movement
about people feeling trapped. Before war there were
Rubik's Cubes. This poem isn't about pain per se. If you pay
attention, the stickers will not appear again, agony will.

I turned down the road where one rarely feels
heroic: husk, shadow, and exit wound.
What I carry: Gregor Samsa, a Volkswagen
(Hitler invented the Beetle, me).

It's a matter of degrees,
the scream, the e(i)ther/or(e),
the hatchet in the knee
    of   now.
    The road, hidden and everywhere,
won't whisper we're here, alone or also alone
in great crowds, to transform, to hop(e) on
the next thing coming.

What we bid: a body over a bridge,
the promise of one-wing, astonishing, what we fall
for, a "chemical imbalance," on TV, *The Price is Right*,
the soul, one dollar, circa 1983.

VIII

Tomorrow, bridge without water.
As if thirst might be met, as if 1,000 *as ifs* could ease
orphaned lips.

Tomorrow without morrow.
This time I might not be playing Dig Dug when you
die, I might not hurt so much
if I hurt first.

Could very well forget to flower.
Tomorrow, a pamphlet peddled in the JFK airport
where clarity doesn't come so much
as surrender, where I'll walk through my own onset
until I face
the door of what I've done.

IX

    I caress my S-drive which holds what's left
of her, my memory—all 3 MB of her. Her vulva
only opening in Acrobat Reader 4.0, her hair still
snaked around my drain. Reared from my living
room, she'd dance and land such blows—
I was afraid she would g(r)o(w)…

    I caress my S-drive which holds what's left
of her. What wasn't saved makes an ocean, an ocean
without waves, storm without eye, 33 fathoms
of forget-me-nots, but still there is the memory
of milk, the little thrill of things gone wrong,
and the Ctrl-Alt-Deletes of our love.

    I fail to save and lose all I worked for.
I'll never touch that torso of mist; the bull of my
ego still stands in a field where a girl runs her hand
over wheat, as if it were inevitability, she will grow
into woman, into sun—
              without weight she will drown.

    And female is the soul of her absence.
    And female is my own soul.

X

"Jesus! We need more balloons."
Maybe the Holy Ghost came down and no one noticed.
Maybe a war or a dead deer. Maybe it's simply a matter
of more balloons. I always wanted the USA
to lose. All my pets left or died because I forgot
to feed them. The genius of "Go balloons" is it implies
both freedom and competition —
a dream tied to a string.

How whales cut doves to lie down in.
How the tiniest birds make the prettiest pillows.
How hovering over every name reveals an avatar,
an image disguised to hide the I —
We drive to work listening to trapped miners
on the radio.

Maybe balloons were bent into the shapes
of familiar animals, maybe if I close my eyes,
there's no more war. They say one of the miners sat up
and said to no one in particular,
"Who's winning?"

XI

    I met a ninja
on an elevator and he embraced me.
X, variable (throwing star), the scar I couldn't see said
whoever finds him (a translation of skin)
will not remember him.

    This ninja was my uncle. Today, on touching
his name, my hands have entered his age
as a body into a blue tarp covering a pool.
And out of that same wake
a delta (Δ, δ) in the eye of the son:
a trine between the 2.

          "I got married,"
he tells me. Remember the neighbor girl you played
Marco Polo with, who died in a car crash. Playing
House without a house. She's married.
            "To have a wife…" he can say.

   A late, florid style of water
      made us want to play
Sharks and Minnows, resuscitation
of a drowned-man, but just joshing, candidly, like he liked
            to do.

XII

I escape a tsunami in the soul, the kind
without telethons. I spray-paint RADIO FETUS
on every bridge in Pennsylvania. I pray *Project
Runway* never ends; I need the thread, pinprick,
thistle of blood, empty spool.

I'm making a scarecrow. Now sell me
your kerosene. Sell me your singe. I want
these crows in my kitchen to cry, to hang
out their white tongues like hotel towels.

I've always enjoyed burning
leaves, little hands, serotine smoke,
the cracked sound of hope, each husk
sowed with its voice.

XIII

I think of your sex.
With dumb-downed heart I think of your sex
as ants hijack the day's blonde daughter.
Even the Pope gets the hiccups.
The cardinal fluttering against the glass:
phoenix, arrested.

I think of your sex, wave which knocks
out the breath, holds a body under, no way to say
which way is up. Death keeps feeding coins
into the meter of your mouth.
O, Consequence,
I am thinking too, about you, free animal
who takes pleasure where she wants, because she can.

O, honey of daughterless dusk.
O, hoarse voice of lightning.

Rudderowstarkweathersampson!

XIV

Let me explain. My dog is dead, no home
or work. My alarm clock is a woman with a shotgun.

I travel by way of trapeze.

Exxon station (stolen): Corona, Jesus, comb-over, Post-Its®.

The state of N. C. allows me to bake 33 oz's of cookies
every Christmas for my friend on Death Row.

Your ass, a pineapple with no knife.

You must have me mistaken for someone else.

Redonkulous.

Dementia.

I have traveled from Pittsboro to New York
where I make minimum wage, and only one soul to sell.

XV

In the racquetball court we made love, God watched
through a tiny square window. A janitor weeping in the dark.
We went to Sheets for Super Nachos and a mixture of all the sodas.
A CEO sprained his ankle slipping on the spot our sex made.

You slept in the shape of the number 3, and left
like a tooth beneath a pillow. I went back to the racquetball
court with your ghostmoney, I read a book
of poems in French amid all your gentle points.
The same old story—a boy and girl in love: somebody's
gonna end up crying on a racquetball court.

I've watched hours of home movies
about how the light came in our kitchen, it was you,
scant anvil, white fire, coming in and out of rooms.

But tonight there's no you; the rain just rains
its awful stammer, I, I, I suddenly start to…
Two doors open and two doors close, a life
spent trying to make the number 3
shadow   enters   shadow.

XVI

    I have faith in being wrong.
Gimmee, customized Hummer, your virgin
rightness, set my odometer to zeros on the left.
And you, Dream, gimmee your mindless
zirconium, your innumerable dishwashing speeds.

    I have faith in being wrong.
A woman with warhead breasts advances—
a courtroom scene unfolds in Hi-def; I am
      convicted.

    The mini-helicopter on my dunce cap flew me
out of the fifth-grade. Congratulations
lice, you've reached 1,000 feet! A bird's-eye view
of the American flag, or perhaps a red-headed kid
mid-noogie. The vice principal is pulling
down the state flag, the one with my face being erased.

    I have faith that I might be
and that I've been less.

    Hey, at least it's a start.

XVII

    This banana clip was emptied on a single cloud
shaped like a gazelle. No one
noticed it in the sky, what with the civil war
on, and me sitting in a field of sunflowers muttering
abracadabras.

    The Tomorrow lost its father,
shaved and took off its shoes.
Shotgun barrels loaded with Prozac®—
nobody said there'd be bread.

    Would there be less pain if we had no face?
The thieves would have a field day on eBay.
There's no way to exaggerate a cucumber sandwich.
The point is—green is perfect.

    Use love's napkin. Use it for abortionburgers.
Use it for the ketchup of car-crashes,
the inner-child's missing balloon,
my 21 bullets for the next shape you take.

       Banana! Banana!

XVIII

It wasn't exactly prison sex, but
I was arrested in the South Square Mall
where I fell in love with those 4 walls
that always = the same story.

Sweet keeper of innumerable keys,
if only you were with me, if only you could see
at what hour these walls become 3. Against
them, with you, we both would be
2, more 2 than anything's ever been. Maybe
I wouldn't even weep as mall security
consults those who've hurt me most,
just keep thinking: *rescue, rescue.*

How I barely hang on,
my right, serving for both arms,
raised, searching for some semblance
of bridge, something to save me
from the lip of alone, the quiet
confession — the word
(home)   is your home.

XIX

    The alarm clock is confused,
bursting into birds.

    Work would not accept my excuse, even
when a goldfinch shot from my pocket, even when
my body became a meadow, a helicopter searching
my skin for something on the loose.

    Enter the ecumenical machine.
O Firewall, allow the alarm-clock birds,
allow the meadow-me. *This* is as religious as I get,
like the inside of water, where my sister's blood
goes, where my uncle ended, where I skipped
a stone and knew I would die.

    Was it a dream or an answering machine
that said our hog, Holy Ghost, was found in a tree
in Siler City, and a litter of blind things beneath
our double-wide was trembling and in need of names?

    Either/or, we were safe, huddled under
an electric blanket nicknamed "The Shield," until an adult
or a sonic cue tore through our torpor with responsibility.

    The birds have become confused,
flowing back to form an alarm clock.

XX

There is a precise moment in every child's life
when they must dismantle a TV to see what little gods
live inside. For me, there were 3. Useless to Krazy glue
a fuse, burnt-hued tubes, the soul, a cathode ray.

Winos would sit in the woods and watch
those TVs. I left them your old shoe. O to walk
across that black glass, shimmering in the almost
sun. All those soap operas set
                                                    free,
all those dead leaves waiting for someone
to walk on them, in other words, any dream
in the shape of an effigy of hands.

I suffer. Is that okay to say? I was talking
to the poem ANYWAY.

In the only play I was ever in, I acted
the fool, the boy who didn't know he was dead.
I was so beautiful the King Lear dude went blind,
I affected a vocabulary of N.W.A, the one
shoe, my wardrobe touch.

Only my beard separates me from you.
You, who could fix anything — will break (you'll teach
me), the simple machinery. Fools, without
a play: your dress rehearsals of drowning, me dancing
in a forest of shattered TVs. All that glass
                        shining in the sun, fool's
                                    go d
                                      l

XXI

How can a "last breath" be a cliché?
He died in December, December died a little too,
its mediocre ad-copy, its well of infinite sadness.
And who's buying it — December, with its pyramid
scheme of belief. "They've filled the well with sand."

I deremember him. In the film *Grizzly Man*,
a man is eaten by a bear. Metaphors are no
match for bears. December is both bear
and metaphor. I'd like to make a rug of regret,
reverse my inner-mink coat.

I reremember him. And today December returns
childlike, as if ashamed its bike was stolen,
blubbering my-bads and humiliation.

And the ocean pretends to be small, to be
changed, as if she loved you, as if some singing
might make a dent. No one notices a tear
in the ocean. Believe me, I've tried
on all your skins of indifference.

XXII

At the end, even the SARS Czar was looking
for me, maker of masks. I haven't written the book
they will throw at me yet. I had "the" haircut,
one shoe, a watch with a game instead of hands.
They dragged me out from under the bridge on national TV.

When the watch broke, I couldn't get the lead balls to fall
down the wells anymore—
they just hung on the lip like a sentence begging
itself not to know its end by who knows
what emendations.

"I'll be the Judge Judy of that," I want
to say to the DA, but I know my fate is a remote
control boat in a sink, the batteries,
almost dead. Are you happy now, you have me.
You have what no one wants, my disease.
I'll draw from where there may not be a me.
I'll exit from my bipolar heirlooms and other sumps,
cemeteries of want
to level and love.

In such states we always turn to oppose
whatever enters from the other side.
Now, a prisoner of too much time,
I lie, or maybe I mean I hang, maybe I'm asking
for it. Either way, here I am.

XXIII

In seventh grade, I couldn't find the heart
on a 3D anatomy model, I just stood there like a town
dotted with paralyzed tornados, as the students snickered
I imagined Andre the Giant flying through the air, I imagined
getting head from Stacy Kerkoff beneath the bleachers.

Today, I brush back the harshness of because
like an angry bee circling a Coke can.
A photo of whales on your phone will not protect you.
Once you enter, you're subject
to the rules, physics of splay, thigh, a list of things
that will die without rain: chickenfeed, angiosperm,
jalapeño seeds... I can say anything—you don't believe me?
A 14-year-old boy rigged 7 TVs in his room
to show his uncle bleeding a hog from different angles,
then invited over a girl named Susan.   See.

Whatever you do, don't believe
this poem. Don't listen to me, my tears won't dissolve
your rings or diamond telephones. Maybe I was high.
Maybe just because. Maybe it's the war. An excuse to use
my harpoon gun, to say "grub worm," "sub-sub librarian,"
maybe it was all just for fun.

I can't get out of my head what Kanye West said after the flood,
your ear pressed against my chest, the little dream
destined to discombobulate a shrink, your hands typing,
your index finger searching for the source
like a failed lion tamer contemplating a chair.
This is the real war—memory, the distance between
animal and thing, the proof, the trick, a matter
of simple anatomy, between the dick
and the brain, lies
the heart.

XXIV

"People die *at* 7-Elevens too,"
two Jehovah's Witnesses, half awake,
weeping incredulously into their coffee.

NPR informs me an American's won
the Nobel Prize in Economics for saying, basically
"expectation determines the marketplace." A 4th grader
afraid of the dark, or a high-school boy who just got his heart
broken, could have told you that.

Those Jehovah's Witnesses deserved a Nobel Prize
for weeping incredulously into their coffee,
and before the sun even had a chance
to shine, on what just happened
to be

a Tuesday.

XXV

　　Magic can't be black, no degree
to disappear in, see me in a sea
of melted vinyl, a vessel of music
is this: think sing and enter:

　　No lees for these storms on the inside,
thrashing night's pale ash and promise
of better-than-befores. Who isn't a crow
squabbling for their piece of meat, who
isn't meat? Faith's based on the delicacy of wrists,
when it should be the snot on the sleeve.

　　There are only two colors,
the way all water flows to the sea.
They buried him in his only suit, the sleeves
too long like so many things
we forget to dream. At an Ace Hardware store
a boy picks his paint from a sample book, torn
between So Much Waiting or Never Finished.
A beautiful woman will always be sawing
　　a board or a man in half.

　　Magic can't be black, remember the principle
of maybe-he'll-come-back? The scar(ve)s—the blues, greens,
and golds, all these tricks he still holds
　　up his sleeves.

XXVI

Season without warning, dumb ribbon,
fistfuls of rope, weather-or-knots, flag at half
                    mast,
broken toys and heroes beckon the black grass,
the halves and the have-knots, crowd beauty
beauty crowds you back.

Fracking laws and loopholes
taught us water is winning.
Hierarchy of hope: *Swimming
for Dummies*. Think of this
as the Cliffs Notes to the book:
"Beauty is just a series of essays
proving that beauty doesn't exist."
A thesis of you leaving me —

Renegade season, you bare
ly break inside me, trapped in a tri
angle of want, a radio, pretty laws
of physics, the high seas, no word
of ransom, no frequency, wave

                    goodbye.

XXVII

A good memory is hard to find.
My dad made us chorizo. I tried to fly
through the TV. My dad scares me.
Ghosts live in the refrigerator. The hearts in there
are ersatzbutter. Someone unmelt me.

Let's not go in. It scares me, this open
door policy. To save ourselves, we balled up
like rollie pollies in the hallways during tornado drills.
"Darker than the inside of a cow," Mrs. Lawson said
straight to my face.

The "whitehouse" is what we called it. I had nightmares
that should have made me a millionaire. They found me
beneath the X-mas tree, literally. My child psychiatrist
became a household name.

Dad, history buff, hailed Hitler's missing testicle,
what survived the fire, but couldn't tell us shit
about the flood. In our house there were no dogs
or gods allowed. Yelling is a sign of exuberance. The good son
didn't get jack if memory serves. Hallelujah for that.

XXVIII

The words *mortgage* and *nightmare* stem
from the same root. Amaranth. I misread Thoreau's
"where now was only water" as "where now
was only *war*." I cut the stems of green
roses you gave me just before
they bud, just so I could say
"premorse of love."

"Chewing your food" could save your life,
or so says my chemistry book, in Guantanamo bay
a prisoner died from "refusing to chew." According
to inside sources, water-boarding
"simulates" drowning
in a "controlled" environment.

Oh, so this is a POLITICAL poem.
Weary like a rose. Another maudlin display
of what cuts and its corresponding degree
of convenience. The fear of fear
has a fantastic name...omitted of course
on behalf of beauty and what we know
we don't know. Close your eyes
and click your heels: "There's no place like
poem."

We are all in a show called *Dirt*—
plundered, downloaded, sold,
where the heirloom of spoons
doesn't reach the mouth that cries:
the wretchedness of love,
an infomercial for knives.

XXIX

Every future ends, bottled
in what wasn't: starfruit, a wedding in June.

Water is beautiful because it is water,
that's it—better yet to feel it on my wrists, without
even a name. Any sustained love amazes me, any innocuous
kiss; I'd rather drown in something I can pour.

Poor fool in the forest dancing, poor little boy
on a string, at what point will he break, what knot of war?

Moon, take this useless armor from my equator.

XXX

Have you ever seen a moment
running from fire, the most tender flesh, always
seconds away, desire, the history of lifted dresses
I pinch in this kick-ass chili
at 2 in the cruel cruel afternoon.

Even the edge has its edge, its bit
lip; molest comes from the root—to touch.
When it's cold and quiet, I like to adjust
the satellite of your sex, we come
closest when we don the properties of planets.

Spoon, black dishwater of us,
stainless steel sink,
all this runoff, the useless condom, splatter of crass
and shun, it's a matter of fractions, the brutal instruments,
                    the cruel life, the hum.
Shhh. Lie back. It will be so…

XXXI

Hope cries uncle, kung fu gripped.

"I don't want to be white anymore,"
I told my mom and dad on national TV.
I signed my name X. *What can brown do for you?*
Imagine De La Soul's laundry.
Will the senator from Ohio please remove his foam finger?

Hope is a Christian. Not needing hope.
Little League games decided by His indivisible hand.
Golf, on the other hand, is luck. All evil
comes from loving God, says God
in the form of Richard Dawkins.

I used to pray to Optimus Prime,
semi-trailer truck of love, a secular
awesomeness that can only be compared
        to Chewbacca,
1986, its omnipotent grillwork died. Hope
head-locked, noogied, and no amount of wookies
could bring back the X-mas presents
I found in my mom's closet.

Lord, all I'm asking for is a sign —
preferably, under the table.

XXXII

    999 calories.
Rimbaud chugging Robitussin®, no trapeze please.
Guillotine the scone-slingers of the ghettos.
Graft an eardrum to the mirror.

    Lucky iceberg. No Dogs Allowed!
Lucky memory that has its cake and eats it too.
Lucky dream of the jouster.

    1,000 calories.
Weightless, the gringo's imagination
slouches towards whatever.
The impoverished sun begs to barter its albatross
for some bread. Buurrrrrrrrr, it's cold.

Cereal stains my tender chapbook.
The sad flag of tarnation waves away.
A streetcar named Disdain.

    Air, air, where!
The corpse minus a calorie = love.
        I dig a hole in the air.

    When Jesus died—thirty three trillion three
hundred thirty three calories.

XXXIII

    If it wasn't raining, I would pull out
like we were taught not to do in Health & P.E.,
nothing between you and me. As if nothing
had a choice, as if you were capable of waiting—
ruin would be our ark.

    I'm naked, primary and cold. At your
feet, a spool of red thread from my wrist.
Two drops of hot milk, mother of nothing,
you were built for this—typing, sewing
my side to your side. Neil Young
knows nothing about needles, holes,
the barracudas of your soul, so let go
of my throat, the language you call
latex. What protects you from the world—oh
                 good, you're making a coat.

    I am the tree that falls
in the forest with no one around. For the record,
I didn't make a sound.

    But it *is* raining. And what has yet to come
will never come, but what has arrived is already gone,
but what has arrived is already gone.

XXXIV

Stranger by my side, pixilated when I attempt
to print—I knew this bar code tattoo would make me less lonely.
When I arrive at airports, no one waits for me, no one knows
my name.

Stranger, stranger still, the ease with which
we bleed, travel through the archipelagos of action
which meet the needs able to provide a bay—
a thing to throw tea into.

Stranger estranged, your code of naiveté
allows you to come closer, your way
of never having to stay
alone.

Stranger inside me, hording
back taxes, texts, and to-do lists
as if anything could be saved, as if it might add up
to a life—little bitch of the IRS, and for this reason alone,
having been born.

XXXV

Shark-jumped episode of another's lover,
all seasons at once. Gimmie the details, tucked
under her one-wing, a *TV Guide*, so violent,
so impossibly paper.

Lunch scene in soap-opera light,
the special, 32, "coldest stuff
in town." The lyric and nervous beer
by her side, as a line of white ants
gnaw on her breasts, whispering,
"She who gives the least shit holds
the key to the world in her hands."

Tables are set with water, dishes
break, actors change names, and stories
never end — fields, skeleton skies, stark,
fallowed, inside, growing like eyes
in the dark.

Woman who, without even thinking,
starts a series of immutable sparks, turns
loose words as tender as baby animals,
which will be raised and served.

And without blocking or make-up,
Lolitas me to pieces, slips away, the needle
of someday setting me back to zero.

So I leave with my side unsown, one
more glass and I'll be gone. Better make it
strong, it takes a long time to get

so alone.

XXXVI

     What good is a wooden horse without an army
inside, or without a war on the outside? We make up
the middle. A YouTube video of Saddam falling through the floor
is not a metaphor. The way us fucking is us fucking.
You won, it's over, climb out of your horse, I'll pay
the millions I owe in what will never flower.

     Are you that way, Helen?
You hardly act crippled, pantomiming a beehive
in public. What army hides inside you?
The grass you lie down in
turns brown, Helen, eves, robes fall
from your shoulders and you can't even see
I appear as 114 snowflakes
martyred in your eyelashes.

     A skinny teenager working at a Dairy Queen in Arizona
feels a letter opener in her ribs the instant
I enter you, and you, who knew you'd become air
know nothing about w(h)a(i)ling, cotton, fait
accompli, unaware of the war around you,
lassoer of ctenophore, lassoer of escaped
ellipsis   …   …

     I count on contact
juice, trap doors and rough drafts of desire,
"what we suppress to arrive at where we are,"
I came in the body of a horse. Oiled waist, your name
means "torch." I burn so you can see.
No one knows what happened
to the men in the belly.

     But I just happen to know you don't kiss
with your eyes closed. Never shoot
                      a gift horse in the mouth.

XXXVII

     So I confessed (to my Boba Fett
action figure) I loved a girl
I do not know. Her mother and brothers tangled
in the string of squibs between cruelty and duty,
a life built on "preemptive strikes."

     Just as I notarized a conglomeration of boy
and man, they marooned me with the memory
of swimming. Her body became a cay, longing
to touch more than just another body
of water, a way out, a strait.

     A toy cannot console, no matter how well constructed,
like _____, outgrown, destroyed by the terror
to attain. I tied my G. I. Joes to our bumper,
microwaved He-Men, left Boba Fett in the well—
it was the religion I craved, the suffering
of all my loves,
                     toys.

XXXVIII

Every Easter we'd hunt for chocolate
Albert Camuses. We deemed it "the religion of teeth," our future
mouths governed by mathematics, syllogistically, each cavity
I have felt and forgotten.

Every letter wants to become number, a new
plurality, "a measure of music," Camus would call it
as we gnashed his milky skull before it melted
into an Apollonian torso of cocoa on a child's face.

So what if the heart always opens
to the same 2 or 3 images; what we need
is a new number, 1 between 2 and 3 for the heart
that's green. My other brother died in an abortion.
Numbers, names, things that never came, we carry like teeth,
with us, after dirt, after mathematics, surrounded by the soft parts
that protect us. For me, it was the dead bees in the bathtub —
the living one, still struggling in her bush.

Memory, 2013's device of the year!
It is Easter, fuck anything for coming back —
we grow baby teeth, born to fall out
and simply stay that way. Here's a dollar.
Now please, just leave me alone.

XXXIX

    Hail, Hail, the kid can swim!
So I float. So I kick
and scream for no other reason
than being born. I scream even more, you're
all here to see me bleed, run down roosters,
bees, the buoyancy of already gone, I was just playing
FISH OUT OF WATER.

    Not even the Newspaper could save
what wasn't dead—thin dream of in-roads, delivered
in a VW bus, the quick-kiss politics of a darkroom,
negatives held to a prodigal son. Born before
the war, my ear pressed to the door, to the noise
that says, since 1986, no two people have truly had sex.

    We whored our pool via free advertising. Paid
through the nose. "Above ground" is a term I still
don't understand. We all come out swimming. Not a life-
guard for miles. They called me White Lightning
in the stands, but nobody knew my name
was Doubled-Over, that I peed my pants
simply to stay warm. What can you do?

    I too want to walk away, but my fans
keep screaming, giddy, selfish, angelic:

    RUN, SAM, RUN

XL

Who would vote against a mascot
like that, unreal handshake, sober and taxless
love, with the properties of a blow-up sheep?
Call me the grocery-store assassin; I'll murder you
with anchors in the name of the Patriot Act,
 in the name of my name.

Think how much we might have minorly annoyed each other,
and fought, and made up, and you know…each thinking
we just fucked the other.

Who could imagine a campaign of ideas
and wristblood would have won out? It's still not clear
what happens after these Disney Dollars are cashed in, but hot damn
I'm gonna pimp this free button they handed out:
          "Try Privacy?"

We might have pulled out—wars, wombs, whatever.
Buried in arrows and bullets
of this ache that we try to write-off as wings,
then fold when forced to produce receipts.
It's not as easy as you think to prove we even live—
the state takes paper, what the soul
          doesn't know.

XLI

    Death playing opossum
spills its fake blood in the real astroturf.
It smells of Guarantee.
That's just, like, your opinion, man.

    Serial killers swear by Mop-n-Glo, talk
under their breath…did you hear that—it came
from the trunk. Someone whistling the theme
to *The Andy Griffith Show* with their eyes
closed—the age-old question: *Revolver* or *Rubber Soul*?
We will miss your twenty-three ribs, no bones
about it, we'll miss your bunched-up amoebas,
your exquisite receipts,
the entire file on you.

    Tarzan will teach the future more than any state
of the union address. I used to think a police state
was like New Jersey or Arizona, without the crime.
When I was being beat with that stick, I kept thinking
about my mouth on your breast, about staying
absolutely still, "Move along," said the cop,
tit
for
tat.

XLII

Weight. And begin again. This time I will tell you
everything. Weight. Let these panic attacks pass, subsidiaries
of more viable storms. Weight. And begin again.

"Who do you think you are hiding from," says the King
of Broken Water, "when you're no longer needed?"

Who needs watching, waiting, pinetree, gone.

I haven't even told you the best part.
I'm nine years old again. The first time I played hearts
I shot the moon. Blood on the back of his hand.

Even the desert felt deserted when he left it.

No one has seen a thing. My soul goal
is to keep your shoulder blades ungoogleable.
In physics, your right leg is what is known
as a "gravity well," or in Pittsboro, "some dark holler."

It wasn't searching so much as falling
that brought me here. Exact music almost
always disappoints me, "they sang in voices more
like angels watching."

I feel better. Deader. Weight. Without. Weight.
Fall. Chappaqua. Nothing leaves me, nothing hides...
Weight, where are you going, the King of Broken
Water has spoken, and it sounded like a sprinkler.

Weight. And begin again. This time I'll tell you
everything. It was just a game we made up the rules to
as we went along.

Come on, it isn't funny anymore —
open your eyes.

XLIII

    Perhaps it moves toward you.
Perhaps madrigals.
Caress it. Say nothing, or night honey. It calcifies
from what clings to it.
Caress it. Seriously, nobody has to know.

    Do not offer it coffee.
Do not mace it. Do not step back
when it approaches as an apparatus of flame,
an animal that has learned to leave... Yes?
Yes. Caress it. No questions asked.

    Perhaps it moves toward you...in order to.
Ever counted each pore on your skin that only
allows exit and that only allows entrance?
Caress it. Don't be afraid. But whatever you do,
don't let it know I sent you. Now go—
what are you waiting for?

XLIV

The computer travels inward,
feminine, without the luxury of salt;
it breastfeeds itself in the fetal position,
screwed together by seven dream-bits.

It Restarts. Flies through wire, wants
to be blood, goes underground, a life
without eyes—hacked, mushrooming
with desire.

Sometimes its tubes burn out
and the equivalent of its eyes
eclipse; a micro-chip isn't afraid
of death, but of losing its memory.

Computer, who does your spywear protect,
with your password that saddens me,
with my longing that indulges you?

Oooh—remember to save me too.

XLV

I can no longer remember the smell of the sea,
even when the waves crash at my feet, even in this poem.

Let us always be leaving each other. Let us make it
a state. Not like North Carolina with its disappearing light-
house, its piers pretending to be bridges. A state
chemically expressed as pressed lips. Your wakeless
epicenter—saline, sulfur, words I say
to remember.

In the future, I will purchase
the ocean like everything else, drown what
we forget.

And if in this way we crash
into the chalked-outlines of each other, we'll cover
ourselves in the electric blankets of having nothing,
and clone ourselves a wombless daughter,
and with what looks like a wing
we will hoist a sail,
and with the breeze at our backs, coast
into the beautiful argument.

XLVI

    We played D&D the night he fell
into a "well" darker than imagination, wide
open like a baby bird mid-cry, blind, waiting
to swallow what sustenance from an un-
      seamed sky.

    Certain shames advance when gaming
in their *Tetris* marathons and their 1,000
turning-aways. Or his left leg, full of food,
that on its own accord, refused to be water,
      anchor, wing.

    So the ghosts get their way, what's new,
mocking even the metaphor of baby bird,
but I suppose I would too.

    I cave, carve myself a cage, because there's
no courage in serving one's self.
Christ! Who falls into fucking wells anyway?
      Lyric poetry.

XLVII

    No one drowned
in the making of this poem.

    We all have a job. A life-
guard, a parking attendant: I have done
these things, and as Employee of the Century
I have also gotten high and lied
in the grass, looking up, expecting
to see many, many things. My degree
in something-or-other.

    Seeing so many waves, so many breaks,
"the surfer grabs his board and goes,"
un-fledged, without shoulder blades, saline, or
midwives hollering, "It's always not quite time."

    The problem with parking lots is
the absolute, the infinite. The problem
with sand is it gets caught in the cogs,
the dreams that weigh anyone down.

    In the prototype nightmare,
I'm stabbed through the spleen, hands
too small to grab hold of the soul, anything
that floats, bound to drown,
being already, so holy.

XLVIII

Now I have 70 questions for the soul.
I have a handful of change, which sounds like the answer
for the first 69.
That there is water inside the sun means nothing
here, here, and here. A Polaroid going up
in flames, chartreuse lament, a chemical
                                    reaction,
in the eyes, not a fire in the whole sun.

    The number 69 knows 70 is blind;
this is no train to ride; this will not get anyone
to their baby. Numbers know any distance
is the same. Two points. A lack of adequate trains.

    Firecrackers go off all night
on the 4th of July. A metaphor for war
or ____? The silence between is like a baby
screaming. All of this comes from some song.
There can be no birds around a ship
in a bottle. Wonder what those black pellets
that when lit, grow and grow (into snakes)
are supposed to represent—
                        an entire life?

XLIX

Muzzle of anxiety, cataract
and crux, tormented by hips, the email ends:
            "We can never touch, okay?"
No search parties are sent, and who'd recognize me,
when even I have forgotten
           the bones of my face.

Which is why I smile at the scene in *Jesus' Son*
with a hunting knife in the eye, the insane search
           for the already found.

Please, please, open just for me
           your unscrawled leaves,
I want to see the 1 without the 3,
I want to jimmy the just-for-you, to know, at least
           what it's like.

But backstage, where we undress, rehearse
how not-to—no audience or applause—only leaves
           waiting to rise.
And clothes, ghosting away,
the silhouettes they cut, float
           down to the cautious hue,
down to the river branches, for a place to lie,
to be unsown, little white leaves, little belly-ups,
at last, right down to the bone!

L

The hammer, the afterbirth, the anvil, the ink,
the already-not-yet, the aperture, the armchair, the pleasure
of cellar door, the chimera, the never, the more,
the bullet, the born, the there, the uncle,
the surrogate, the peninsula, the risen,
the drown, the jig-saw, the Jew, the glass,
the ceasefire, the phonograph, the smoke.

    Immutable, external, hungry,
lithographed, indexed, widowed, thirtytwoed,
tumescent, deracinated, alive.

    Snowing, burning, ballooning,
pelting, sapling, fasting, inoculating,
lying, weeping, a tiger, snowing, snowing.

    Almost, right here, beyond,
perhaps, during, to the left of, so much, after,
distant, always, this one, almost, never, too much.

    The succulent, the air, the quickening,
the kiss, the august,
the rebuff, the rope, the cruelty, the spittle,
the punchline, the rags, the reckoning,
the 1-wing, the awl, the would-be breasts,
the water, the lessness,   the wait.

LI

A lie. I was just kidding,
that's all. No biggie. Besides
would you really want to know
how much it hurts when someone you love dies.

A lie. Just between us.
It's cool. Keep it on the DL.
Like when you played opossum by the pool
pretending to pump water from your lungs. After
I saw *Batman*, I thought that moth-thing I saved
in the net of the leaf-skimmer might have been you.

And me, who you saw cry when I couldn't kill
the rooster you raised,
and you, walking away, when I didn't believe you could fly;
a stalemate, you taught me, was in a game when
neither player can kill the other's king.
But I was just pretending to cry.
So there.

So now you know—it was all a lie.
And if you want to keep on dying, feel free.
Next time I won't even watch you when you play.

LII

Because in every story something is lost
and found, I know this is a poem —
junkyard of the just gone.

At exactly what point did the you
and the you and the you become the me? Where was I
when the condom, the loved one, and the missing
shoe fused into a liquid statue of don't-look-at-me?
Who needs magic in a city of embraceable wolves?
I'll always own the memory of pain, the channel
where I harbor between the trachea and the heart,
that wants and does not want its color, the sea
endured, green, green.

Because there is a person composed entirely
of my broken parts, because all that is left is a JPEG
named BLOWNTOSMITHEREENS.

So this is your story, which acts
as both table and effigy, at the edge
of beauty, it quivers, it sings, it holds
        no water.

LIII

Who screams that eleven isn't twelve o'clock!
As if numbers could commiserate: two divided by
two = the blues, Robert Johnson, born at 22.

Burt Reynolds in *Boogie Nights*, the father
of lost souls. A toupee of thorns. Too many sins
to trespass, a family is a recognized religion. Pain, betrayal,
selfishness: imagine love without such measurements.
There is a life beneath bridges that makes crossing a river
without getting wet seem blasphemous. The Hungarians had
human dams. Thank you for your sons and daughters,
Burt Reynolds.

You see what it is to be without is, ownership
of tenselessness, you see what a family must endure,
like it or not.
You see all this grease on the elbows
just to reach the mouth.

LIV

Zoomania, mineral, animal, "They can squeeze
their bodies to the size of a pencil." Little nidus of doubt,
oscillation and wave, fuck physics, love gets in
through the cracks. De-fenced.

Sometimes I hit against all the againsts,
at the moment I'm masturbating, becoming
blacker and blacker, almost sun, almost son.
There is a history professor in my eyelids jotting
everything down — another Arizona resurrected
in my 7th true rib. Oxygen visits its alma mater,
what won't burn burns, and even the eyes
will bleed over time, even the blood.

I took my dart once
and pointed it to your pale neck,
told you how you'd die —
it was lust,
up to the hilt.

LV

Chances are you haven't been born yet, walking around Chappaqua, after all thought, without legs, without adult dreams, cauterized, exhumed, scrawled in the margins of…

 The difference is, skin is porous by design, and always aspiring to a condition of lemon rind. The soul, sponge-like, indifferent to light, functions like a swimming pool pump—it doesn't care if you believe.

You could wash away out there without a shoe, an oar, a chances are. Here, take my GPS. You're going to need a broom for that shattered map, an umbrella for the green and ceaseless precipitation of the heart—so long numbers, so long night, so long lungful
of water, yes you, million pieces……………………………………………
I love you.

LVI

    Even so, I rise, faceless
to the job of being alive. I drink coffee to move
my bowels, to get right my intrinsic lefts. Every day
I grow another face, take another stab
at this living thing, then fall into an endless
abyss of things-to-do.

    A niece could come unstitched with so much happiness,
                so much
cheese toast and language stuck to the roof of the mouth,
as adults, unable to diffuse the flint of lament, wrench
us from dreams of anemones into a tremulous wind—
thrown-back like an adolescent fish, phosphorescent,
wishing the future a thing to float in,
and believing it 'til the lungs burn.

    Fringes of invisible weft,
re-sown womb, Sweet Fire, I never meant to neuter you,
                absence,
clefts, coronation of air, there, at the feet,
The Slave of Water, praying for a vessel.

    Match after match in the dark,
wave after wave in the belly of the spoon.

LVII

    I imagine you
find this book in the woods. You flip
to this page: Here is your curse. White magic.
You always loved a good game, playing with dolls
(this one is you), inventing a new hell.

    Your name is the name of the fear of being found out.
You are hit by a car.
You are broken up with via text message.
You are robbed by a rookie robber who injures himself and sues you.
You write airport fiction.
I am your dentist.
I have hammers for hands.
You wake up with a mouthful of dirt and onions.
Your neighbors are pedophiles and frat houses.
Your dog dies…twice.
Your soul is a white dwarf.
You are buried alive with your fucking iPhone.
Your organs are used for shark chum.
You wake up to a permanent sangria hangover.

    Black hail falls on your daughter's wedding.
Every day the next day is the biggest exam of your life.
When you say "coffee" all people hear is "liquid turkey."
May you be audited…every year
by the person in the world you have wronged most.
You have telethons instead of dreams.
The little black box inside your soul
that records your every action
is handed to the Devil when you die.

The Beginning

LVIII

In the cell they gave us beet salad—
people would die for beet salad.

A man made a naked woman out of Legos he smuggled
in his asshole. She was gray like an ocean. A dream of the ocean.

A York Peppermint Pattie commercial where an old man
is skiing in his living room was all I could think of
when they asked me if I believe
in Heaven. Hell is the same thing. An advertisement
during the '86 Winter Olympics.

My friend/cellmate would pretend his popsicle stick
was Kate Winslet. How he'd pray to that blonde
talented specimen of woodwork. I'm sure I'm not the only one
who heard it… Nobody knows music
like the damned. Our husks healed by
a celebrity splinter, a Lego-snap, the sound of another man
eating beet salad.

I whisper to the guard, "go and listen to the sea."
Put your ear to the bottom of the ocean, can you hear me
breathing through a microphone? That's what history
sounds like.

I no longer snicker at my mother
who is praying in 1988 on a Sunday, at 4 o'clock
for her undead brother,
for the sick, the poor, the imprisoned,
for the soul
of her only son.

LIX

The terrestrial strongbox of love
buried beneath the ground makes the sound
of a toy before the batteries die,
imagine a whirr you can't kill, the conscience
as a series of surrenders.

There's no Internet access in the ocean.
The World Trade Center, inhumanable, perfect
for tight rope walking. Balance is the last act of grace,
the music at the end of any rope. Could be.
Possibly. Maybe.

The strongboxes, b(u)yproducts of the passing
of time, the evolution of disposing the dead—
a hole: a mound: a coffin: a cubical.
My neighbor was wrapped in peanut packaging,
my uncle, ashes in the ocean.
When people die, decisions must be made—
they never found my uncle's other shoe.

My mom says her father's in the 3rd stage
of dying: yes, no, fuck you, I don't want to:
the 3rd stage is *bargaining*, then comes *anger*,
there is a 5th and final stage, but I should warn you,
most of us will die
before we reach *peace*.

LX

"Be an uncarved block of wood," my fans
would shout during tennis matches. My patience,
like my backhand, deaf, often run-around.

Born buck-naked and brave like every other
good-for-nothing boy. Nobody arrived on camels
bearing frankincense or myrrh, instead an Hispanic nurse
brought my mother a chrome rose, stolen
from a dead man's bed. Lungless child exploding
in pidgined silence. I'll die with my diapers on.

I grew up under a constellation of chewed gum.
I dreamed someday I'd take the shape that letters make.
When my uncle died, I was in geometry class
dreaming of battleships that say "I'm sorry" to the sea.
My patience, moth-eaten and thin, defeated by the dream,
fat, ice-cream-chinned, in the corner, grinning a toothless grin.

John Malkovich, Driftwood Sculptor — uncarve me.
Discover my body, a block of buoyant wood. See it
as a swan, the twisted torso of a tennis player. Save
my serve, Mr. Malkovich, my poor toss,
my perfect soul.

LXI

Tonight I get down from my lawnmower.

The same machete mom used to put her make-up on,
her little brother, Mayor of Well Water, will make sing
through the bone of a bird that can't fly
as I try to hide my eyes behind a black grapefruit,
not to mention the sun, blacker than anything.

Dad must be up pragmatizing and perhaps
he'll think I am not lost.
My sisters, washing each other's hair
in bubblish gossip,
preparing for the church of economics
and catcalls, will arrive
fashionably absent.

Numerous family forgotten,
but the house still stands, where everyone is asleep.
Not even the TV is left on, calling us to come home.

I dial my uncle but just get the machine,
a parrot's voice squawking, "Has anyone seen my other shoe?
Has anyone seen my other shoe?"

They are all sleeping in 'til infinity,
and so sweetly, even my lawnmower yawns, dead
tired, it idles, asking forgiveness
of the grass, muttering something like
"everything will be alright" and as the blade slows
in its swivel, and it's almost allowed to sleep—
the other shoe drops.

LXII

          Unnamed,
the girl I lost my virginity to
died while I was getting high — in the carpet,
the baby breathing, washed in the alpenglow
of M.A.S.H., I too, wanted to be enter
tained, me, the deadgirl, the TV, at last, a certain
surrender, a white flag, hoisted
to the music of no apology.

          Sanguine,
the shag, aspiring to grass, a fucking grave
in the living room — remember the flag we made,
dumb, naked and brave. Who else would say,
"victim, kiss me?"

          And from that point, I'll follow you
into that island, and against its shores,
grow a bank of mossy yes for you to rest
your elbows on, and in that way,
help you suffer less.

LXIII

    It rains 32s. Mornings, I'm tired
of pulling your runaway hairs from my mouth.
Hope lashed with numbers, rope,
the unacknowledged country of your-head-on-my-chest,
Darjeeling, lightning that stands still.

    Skies of purple kites trapped in trees,
heart-mollusk crawls to its kill, blonde
skies, wet with a chance
of impossibility.

    The flock, unmoved by a man's hands
swelling into sledge hammers, pecks its cake.

    I save myselves. But the knives
in the trees quiver, the rudderows so still
they approximate water,
and the cricket's screech.

    The sun, hungover and doubled, sinks
into its crisis of will; ceded by sudden
thirst, I go out looking for the perfect 2,
knowing all there ever is, is 3.

LXIV

I desire, against my will, despite these 33 stitches in my wrist, to place a hummingbird on the clavicle of my enemy, dressed in neoclassical pride and a black dress, whispering impossible dates and historical events and like a mixed tape end with a hisssssss.

The heart is green from so much waiting; and the weeping that breeched the levees — I'm talking to you, roots, thresholds, withins!

You, who hunger to shake the public ribcage, who sleep beneath freeways, without the come-on's of capital, without the gutted voice of an automotive city, you, who wish to kiss the face of the AIDS victim, howl at the laws of the 3 known and naked dimensions:

Present   Past   Future

(Go fuck yourselves!)

LXV

    Once and for all I'd like to explain my name —
Sampson, while not directly biblical,
due to that impossible "p" placed like a flower
that blooms once a decade between the "m" and the "s,"
means a beautiful woman
is always coming
to cut my hair.

    It doesn't mean I can feel rain
in my knee, and no, I'm not related
to America's first mass murderer, nor am I Native American —
      unless I am.

    Starkweather rather, is a combination of superhero
and real person —
Superhero: Stark
Historic: weather
Rudderow is a nonsense word made up
    by my mom.

    There is another theory
involving a boat, an oar
an alone
rowing
rowing
rowing

LXVI

I see your dolor, and raise you a fear of water.

When you suffer, in short, from the aesthetics
of a chair, descry Pound's *black bough*! You calypso
into the kitchen, pure ghost, with civic lust
convinced the whole social mechanism
fits into your purse.

The sweetly dead, how lo your gos,
how flawless your float, how did you get so
ghost?

You, dead one, tell your shoulder blades
to shut up, it's too late to reverse
rain, to rise, warm-bodied
out of what aims to be filled,
give up your crown of seaweed.

I see your fear
of water, and before you fold, with gravity
on my side, call: 2 black boughs, heavy
rain, and the king of hearts.

LXVII

By law, I bequeath the oxygen in your lungs.
I am allowed, by the state of Arizona: a memory
of swimming, the torn corners of 5 one-hundred
dollar bills, epaulets, and an expired driver's license.

Chemistry killed you—colors holding
a knife in your brain like a concert: sky, well-water, whatever.

How much uncle remained inside—
etched in carbon, purer than coal, diamond,
Han Solo, like a flower kept way beyond green
because of its emblem, because of its evidence
of everything leaves.

When you told me you walked to Oregon "against your death,"
I thought of Ingmar Bergman playing chess, Niketown,
that computer game I played in the 3rd grade—spoiled meat,
wild and spontaneous fruit. How many times I died
trying to ford the river, never finding out what waited
beyond that water, the story of why we try to cross
the same stupid river, the same fucking game

over.

LXVIII

It is July 44th, according to the microwave
and everyone knows time is green,
digital, and blinking.

A tiny parade is happening inside the rain,
a hydrogen cheerleader rides a float-shaped float,
fistfuls of candy.

*The World Trade Center attack was due
to a lack of imagination.* There will always be
one human who can beat a computer at chess.
There will always be a man wanting to break
a beer bottle over another man's head,
and a rain to wash it away.

We walk with an obscene weight, and with a single
sigh,
our mechanical animal lost electricity,
the time was exactly 12:00 and all the dead
(VCRs) agreed. (Betamax)

And my uncle's painter's hat, it was white,
hanging on the coat-rack, not uttering a sound

a
t
f
u
l
l
m
a
s
t

LXIX

    Dear ocean, what do you want from me, with your saline
machine? How soft in your favorite t-shirt,
how green your water seems.

    You follow a ghost logic, coming in-and-out
of rooms, leaving your skin of oooooo's in the kitchen,
having to hack through your afterbirth to get a beer,
while the waves crash inside the library, the books float
like boats, the taste of tungsten and memories
of little titties, haunted by the constant disguise of "I."

    This is the philosophy of black wings,
the terror of having shoulders inside any body
of water.

    Dear ocean, such a shitty machine,
you can't keep everything—
who we love, we love retro.

LXX

Everyone applauds at the nonchalance with which I sink
to the bottom of things—it's in the genes, loose change and gravity…
this gift of drowning.

Do souls go on without a vessel? Or is there some other
who offers a strait between being and letting go, between anchor
and canoe? Like the woman in the park offering Cheetos to tiny birds.

My uncle weighed 186 pounds when he drowned. Benefactor
of faux stones and well-water—how lucky to have inherited both things
to throw and to be thrown into. I have trouble loving people
when they're still alive. I have a niece now, I have a woman in Texas
who I listen to breathe through speakerphone, I have *Fitzcarraldo*
on DVD, so yes, let the living love the living.

I have very little faith in frequent flyer miles. Everything becoming
numbers. We need a new number. One that will save us like a story
that travels in every direction all at once. Poetry is not words,
it's the decision to go walking, forever, and never stop.

And yet we fear to take another step, coming from a family
that falls into wells, wondering if we'll swim or sing.

LXXI

I am tired of language, the thing between this
and that, the distance we must travel merely to arrive
at a name, the 1,000 doves of within.

Shhh. No one knows what is still inside you…
Shhh. Don't breathe. No one knows the future
and the past do nothing but play
with words all day. Shhh. Don't say…

All these promises, departures, heat.
The simple seeking of water, the shadow
of a girl, kneeling. The grass, sleep. And where
do we go from here, when without
is not a known direction?

Hush too, radio on the inside,
no one is listening. Not even the sun
can tease this excess sugar out of me, this string
of dumb and harmless words, always
attempting to renew, always trying to find you —
and to think, I was going to end this poem
I am tired of love
and to think, I was going to end this poem

LXXII

Forget futurism and its various films, I want to talk to you
without skin, to plant this banter in you, I want the fodder
in leaf, wings to sprout, a delicacy of seedlings, to pull
the perfect root from the past that is half
enough to flower, even too much.

Room with five entrances and zero exits, useless key,
I tied a loose tooth to you, ransacked fire, thought of air
planes, still, only zero manages to be free. The Earth
rotates, and we are barely ever moved, remember
hug the (re)turns.

Love floated down like the dead
in a flood, and there was enough oxygen
for the fire, even too much!

LXXIII

    Another obscene gesture — !@#%$&* — has triumphed. This
is the truth. To question the actual; e.g, I never leave
the house without my lightsaber. The only
snow in Phoenix, Arizona is sin.

    Another obscene gesture !@#%$&* — has triumphed,
anonymously, without a splash. The pool water
in the lungs: chemically pure. An heirloom. My security
deposit, my FICA, paid in full —
                  so I am free
to be green and happy and faithless, to be
the lifejacket, what the bloated body dreams;
my laughtrack — a dead DJ.

    Absurdity, you are purer than pool water.
Absurdity, you are enough to put death in its place.
Oh Absurdity, you are too much.

LXXIV

Invisibility is easy; if I could have one super power
it would be fucking you, or maybe to be you, fucking me.

I'm speaking of own(h)ership, the betweens and in-
sides, the two tiny indecisions of the thighs, the boundary of to-know,
sacrilege, tougher than water, the broken will of any wave.
Inside, we're all made of laughter and exploded feathers —
in the 5th grade, Ms. Lawson pulled a crow from my hair,
which, on being found, thrashed and cried and explained
its shame of being a white bird, of disappearing
into the blankness of thinking, which is why I scream
to crush this machine in my skull, and wish to kiss
the livid throat — the crow that cries from being found.

Super heroes never had to deal with ideas
like these, so it's with this radio lodged in my neck
that I set my frequency to suffer, extract any memory
until I'm alone with the would-be trees,
black forest of vespers and pure thought.
I resettle into someone else's shadow
and in order to feel closer to you —
            touch myself.

LXXV

Bang, bang, you're all alive.

God had a gun. It shot a flag with "BANG!" on it, which somehow seems to support Intelligent Design and all that.

How strange to be alive. Before I was dead, it was my favorite. Life is like a box, with Tom Hanks inside it. You float nothingly behind that hippocampus that like a memory of letting go of lightning bugs into a mason jar, goes from a glow to the nadir of cold glass, until pain is soothed away into the end of a prosthetic limb. When Andre Agassi said *Image is Everything* he could not have known he was making a commercial for God. Death then is the opposite of the image. Original, death®.

Casualties of the pop gun. Orphans of the one word.

And yet the dead are not dead. They float on the ceilings of everything, they come back in their old age wearing earrings like Ed Bradley. They sing "60-Minute Man." They die with a flag to their head.

Bang, bang, you're all alive.

LXXVI

All night long I keep drawing
the charred straw out of your mutest O.

In the name of all the unplanned birds
and the poor soul caught between 2 and 3.

In the name of the stranger I became to her,
lost keychain in the snow, tiny wooden heart.

In the name of her with the deaden(e)d voice
and cords cut, tides and ebullitions inside her,
bound to drown in ebb and argument.

Tide of starfished bodies, torn limb
from limbo, island that always remains
just 99 storms away.

Endings, married in no calendars,
2 days that never come together,
that do not reach the other   ever.

LXXVII

It hails so much, as if to make me surrender
and give up these seeds
I've gathered from the e(a)ves
of every atom.

May this rain never end.
Unless I am allowed to fall
from the same source, unless they bury me
in a downpour, in the waters
that surge from every fire.

This rain, to what end will it reach me?
I'm afraid I'm left with 1 wing dry,
afraid of being alone, without having been tested
in the deserts of impossible vocal chords,
which, like a kind of music,
will be entered, sustained,
always towards a condition of rising,
and don't we in fact rise downward?

Rain, sing into me this ocean.

SELF HELP POEMS

Sampson Starkweather

This is what will happen. We will write a book. The slowest flower in the world will begin to bloom. Our parents will grow old and die of diseases we will surely inherit, and seemingly all at once. Our sisters and brothers, our friends and family will all die. We will rent a car. Head for Brazilia. Bleed our dreams like a 1,000 pound pig. You will die gracefully in the back seat to some music that hasn't been born yet, a map of the desert in your hand, lines scrawled in handwriting I will later tell everyone is the official handwriting of the dead. I will live for 300 more years, and die wrapped in a huge tropical leaf on an island they will name after me, and we will never be forgotten by anyone ever again.

When I was little everything hurt. Not like it hurts now, not like spikes or iron lodged in my skin. It was more like the opposite of a kite, a premonition, like *déjà vu* before you've learned the word, like finding your Christmas presents in the closet. Whenever I felt cheated or disappointed my dad would say, "that's life in the big city." He said it with a kind of glee that made me want to punch him, but even coming from bum-fuck North Carolina, I knew when I grew up, I'd live in that city.

When my dad ran for office, the good old boys slandered him by saying he was a communist and that his son was a poet in New York City. They said it with a venom in their voices that gave them pleasure upon release. When I first heard it, it gave me the chills—is it possible to reach our dreams and not even know it?

My mom sleeps with one of those breathing machines. I tell her it's all in her head. A fear tactic created by marketers to make her spend money. Now I have an irrational fear that she will die in her sleep and I will feel guilty for the rest of my life. I've been eating chocolate before I go to bed because I heard it helps you dream. It seems to be working. Now I just need something for when I wake.

Four days ago you went into the desert. Your voice sounded like you swallowed a bee. I imagine you standing with some bearded man by a Jeep, at the edge, where the road ends and the sand begins, smiling, scared shitless, quoting Keats or Coleridge as the wind picks up, taking the past with it. As if I didn't know you're just a dude with a divorce and bills and bad plumbing and a neighbor who chops wood at night in his underwear. Dreams drive us crazy. You're probably sleeping in some state-of-the-art tent. I hope you didn't get my email telling you how you'd die. I'm sure everything's fine.

Somehow I've managed to avoid speaking, direct eye contact, or personal proximity with my boss for four straight days now. I spent all day Thursday watching YouTube clips of a four-part documentary called: *Predators and their Prey.* There's a bright red light on my office phone that's been there for months. September birthdays are coming up. Needless to say, some sort of reckoning is at hand.

The perfect drug is one you only experience once, and the rest of your life is spent chasing that feeling. After McCain's concession speech I didn't think I could get any higher. But when he was standing in front of 100,000 people talking about the transitive properties of hope, it felt like I was at a once-in-a-lifetime rock concert. The movie we had all been waiting for was finally before us and impossibly better than we imagined, and with each newly delivered line, it kept getting better. There, sitting in my car in the dark listening to that voice coming from the radio, I achieved absolute belief, and it had nothing to do with politics or humanity or any of that shit, it was simply the fact that language did this.

The entire office is crammed in the conference room watching a poor video-feed of the Inauguration in the dark like God was about to tell them what to do. I'm standing outside making copies, giving physics what it wants, listening to the preacher talk about humiliation, history, and hope. He's making future apologies and asking forgiveness for our certain wealth and audacity. It makes me so fucking angry, but I don't know why. Something about those people sitting in the dark, people I work with, tearing up, all this agreed upon, all this false love, this horrible illusion of "us." I am writing this to you from my shitty little cube, wondering how I got this alone, everyone who comprises my adult life huddled around a voice and a freeze-frame of a black limousine.

I saw Mickey Rourke on Charlie Rose last night. He was being held back by his naivety that art is about artistry. Doctors told him he was one punch away from having his life ended, but something wouldn't allow him to give up. His therapist told him he was in a hopeless situation, but still had hope. All humans aspire to the condition of Mickey Rourke.

That phrase "your chosen field" always makes me think of the fields of my youth—the bright green fields of North Carolina in the summer, the brown fallow fields of winter, and those morning fields harvesting fog and god knows what. Fields you'd like to wade out in like water or music, lost in their sweet laws. Memory is a department store. You walk around dazed looking for a field to choose. But it's fucked up, like a dream that ends right before it merges into the real. No one chooses their field. The way it works is, it just happens to you. It's perfect, like the weather. Like this poem.

New York is a vast experiment in loneliness. You know the title of Lorca's masterpiece, *Poet in New York*, was intended to be a joke, an ironic paradox. Where even the pigeons lack souls. Now everyone you meet is a "poet in New York," and the title has become a kind of flag for all these pitiful fools. We've become a skyline unto ourselves.

You live in Texas and I live in New York. Do you ever think about that? Sometimes I wonder how we are not the same person. Have you ever driven late at night on a dark highway in the middle of nowhere, when all of a sudden there is a flood of blinding lights and a handful of construction workers in bright yellow hats and orange reflective vests with welding masks on, operating giant deafening machines, going down into the bottom of the earth, and one of them waves you past, as sparks fly into the night. That's exactly what it's like inside me. All the time.

Remember those fields I invented a few emails ago? Of course you do. Here are the things I culled out: a girl's dress, a bull, wind, barbwire, grass, a chunk of ice, dragonflies, fireweed, gasoline can, a little blood, one cloud, too blue, the sun, the sun. Go, do what you must with them.

Lately, I've been telling people exactly what I want, mean, and feel. Everyone laughs at me, which is appropriate, since I learned this from watching Chris Rock talk shit on that Katrina fund drive. When dumb people think you're a genius, how are you supposed to take that? I tell people exactly how I'm going to hurt them. You realize this is the most important discovery yet for our poetry.

Did you see the moon last night? It was so bright I couldn't masturbate, like the entire world was making a movie about me, documenting my shame. So instead I thought about that Larry Levis poem where the moonlight is so unreal he's afraid it will wake his son, asleep in the next room, who he's about to leave forever, and is trying to conjure the tact and decency to explain it all. It was so bright I swear you could hear it. The saddest organ.

Ironically, that movie *Moonstruck* was on channel 13 last night. The moon is this big symbol of bullshit or hope, but in the end, it doesn't matter because either way it's undeniably there. A family we all belong to. And even though I knew it was coming, I cried at that scene where Nicholas Cage, with that ridiculous chewed-up rubber hand, pleads to Cher in the cold air to come to bed with him: "The stars are perfect. Not us. We are here to ruin ourselves and to break our hearts and love the wrong people and die." My stepmom says my dad doesn't sleep anymore because he's trying not to die—not me, it's just this fucking moonlight that won't shut up.

Literature is more than words. If 100 pages were ripped from the spine of *Don Quixote*, if the pages were warped and rain-damaged, if the ink was smeared, it would still survive. It would still have value for whoever tried to read it. It's like the sea. Familiar and unknown, fecund and unstoppable. It's like how I told you that everyone has a Diet Coke story inside of them.

Did I ever tell you about where I lived in grad school? It was the "business" of this bald, mustached scam-artist Bronx guy who was 6-5, 310 pounds, in this apartment complex in Yonkers, overflowing with the accumulated junk of a life, several marriages, and about two dozen failed business ventures. His scam du jour when I was there was a "grocery delivery service," and get this, the name of his company was Bag Boys. They had t-shirts and supposedly even a TV commercial on local cable access to the tune of the show COPS: *Bag Boys, Bag Boys, watcha gonna do, watcha gonna do when they come for you, Bag Boys...* He had a gang of delinquents working for him including my "homeless" roommate, Dirty Steve, who disappeared one day after stealing a jar of $2 bills and rare coins to do his laundry. When Four-Fingered Eddie from Florida, an alcoholic gambling addict with a silver handle-bar mustache moved in with his motorcycle and sometimes-old-lady Dee, things really got insane. They came to one of my SLC basketball games, drunk and on glue or something worse, and heckled the other team and hooted obscenities at all the SLC goth kids in the stands. I changed my phone number as soon as I left grad school so none of those crazy fucks could ever call me or track me down. I felt like I'd stumbled into a never-ending episode of *the Sopranos* and couldn't get out. It was about a month ago when I finally heard it: I was reading *The Savage Detectives* with the TV on in the background when I looked up to see some commercial which looked like an 80s video game where a pixilated bald man with a shopping cart bounced around the screen like one of those icons when you leave the DVD player on too long, and coming from what sounded like a blown-speaker, *Bag Boys, Bag Boys, whatcha gonna do, whatcha gonna do when we come for you*

I've always said Mike Tyson is my favorite poet. He was on Charlie Rose last night; he's 42 years old now. As Charlie and some indie director were talking about art, he just blurted "malice" out of nowhere, as if it was something he had been thinking about for years and just remembered. Everyone at the table looked as if they thought their life was at stake. Mike leaned back and smiled. There is such a thing as genius of experience, the genius of victimhood, the genius of shame. Then again, a man ain't nothing but a man.

Nobody at the hospital believed me when I told them I got elbowed, they said it looked more like an axe wound. The blood matted in my hair made me look like the Predator, and I purposely left blood to dry on my face so the ER would treat me sooner. The woman said it would be "a l-o-o-n-g wait." I felt like a giant sitting in the waiting room in my little soccer uniform watching *Dancing With the Stars* as blood bubbled from my head. Several families got up and left and one woman kept whispering to her son not to stare. She spoke to him in Spanish when she didn't want me to know what she was saying. She told him I was a bad man and he better not look me in the eye. Luckily for them, my eyes were glued to Belinda Carlisle.

A woman with cancer wailed and moaned and rolled around like an animal, and a 20 year-old mulatto boy, whose face got sliced up in a knife fight, and was told he would never smile again, refused to tell the cops who cut him. The doctors were stressed and sleep-walking, loved ones walked around like confused ghosts. I was sad when they finally wheeled me away. The doctor said I was going to feel this, then pressed an industrial staplegun to my scalp and blasted three staples into my skull. I felt like Mikey Rourke in *The Wrestler*. But not in the Hamletesque depth-of-the-soul sort of way, just in the middle-aged-dude-shot-full-of-metal-staples sort of way.

Have you noticed all the commercials these days are trying to cash in on the economic crisis? In an empty conference room on the 34th floor, there is a whiteboard with the words *accountability, transparency, responsibility, God* written in red sharpie. As if you can build trust simply by coming out and admitting anything. It's a marketing strategy like anything else. I'm afraid our poetry isn't any different. What does a poetics of shame even mean? A manifesto of failure. If only our poems could have a mascot, like a talking gecko with an English accent, or maybe a pile of money with a set of plastic eyes slapped on, if only Rockwell's *Somebody's Watching Me* could be blasting in the background as you read this.

When you texted me that the name of our book would be Brasilia, as in the mythical city the homeless guy was looking for in the Austin Public Library, I misread it as Brahzillia, as in a giant, nationalistic, half-lizard, half-frat-brother Godzillalike monster, that goes around breathing "Sup brah's" like fire, and I saw the cover as this towering, pink-skinned frat boy in cargo shorts and a shell necklace destroying the city, smashing sky scrapers in glacial New Balances, its enormous human shadow blocking out the sun.

Nintendo always felt more real than life. Simple yet somehow beautiful worlds, constantly breaking down, designed, whether intended or not, as pixilated avatars of hope. Old school video games are perfect precisely because of how unreal they are. They don't try to teach you anything, except if you see a hammer, you better grab it.

I've always preferred dictionaries to stories. *A dictionary resembles the world more than a novel, because the world is not a coherent sequence of actions but a constellation of things perceived.* In a dictionary, time does not exist. Lives do not happen in order, we remember at random and often on accident or mistakenly. You are playing tennis on the courts where I grew up, some crazy bandana on your head, laughing and talking poetry, weeds sprouting from the cracks in the court. You are driving from the airport with the windows down, beneath a series of crisscrossing overpasses like giant concrete octopuses, you are taking me to your house for the first and last time in our lives. This is all in the dictionary.

Did I tell you how I Google my uncle at least once a week? Sometimes I add search words to his name like some kind of fucked up equation, Tony Newhall + drown + Phoenix + one-wing. All I ever get is different douchebags' LinkedIn profiles. It's not like I expect to see a home video of him standing in front of a waterfall telling how one leg is full of food and the other is hollow. I'm not naïve. One day he'll come up though, I just know it.

It's true, I live in the woods alone. Sometimes, when I walk out into the dark, I feel I'm going to be pulled in and mauled by some creature. I'm practically waiting for it. When my motion light goes on, I know some animal is approaching. I'm not going to say anything transcendent sounding about how maybe the beast is me. That's not my style.

The woman I told you about who has drunk nothing but Diet Coke for the past 30 years and writes those Fabio-covered historical-romance novels was fired today. She didn't say anything to anyone. I have a copy of her new novel *A Kiss of a Traitor* in my cube, along with her copy of my own book, *City of Moths*, which I've been meaning to sign for her for almost a year. I have a guilt that feels like 30 years worth of Diet Coke sloshing in my gut. It feels good.

I thought you said a field of opposites. What is the opposite of a field anyway, a mountain, a pinprick? My philosophy professor said everything has an opposite. What is the opposite of mid-way? That's where the poem happens.

At a coffee shop in Peekskill I met a Russian novelist and her daughter, a German opera singer, who had just given a performance for three people. Her mother, her mother's boyfriend, and a man who left at intermission. The singer was pleased with her performance but disappointed that there was no audience. Her mother argued that jerking off is a sport. Where everyone wins. The opera singer's lipstick was so red it was the memory of red. In the middle of the coffee shop, like a bank robber who has rehearsed his heist a thousand times, she unleashed an instant aria. I had to check if I was dead. Everyone stopped and applauded, and I knew my poetry would never be the same.

After the aria, everyone in the room felt like James Wright at the end of that poem where he pets the horse. Even though shit like that never happens in real life. Looking out the window at the theater where she had just performed, I noticed below her name on the marquee, in giant letters *The Wrestler.* I shit you not.

The problem with fiction is that it pretends to be real, or is predicated on the idea that there is a real, always attempting to get you to believe. The reason poetry works, "real" poetry, is that it has no pretensions of being real, it doesn't care if you believe, it doesn't even believe in it itself, it *is*, or rather, it is just…language, which, only on its own is perfect, believable, which is what Spicer meant by *the absolutely perfect poem has an infinitely small vocabulary*. Don't get me wrong, the poem wants. It wants more than fiction, more than a starving baby, and goes on, screaming, quietly like a wave in a vacuum, its want, always traveling, internally, monstrously, for lifetimes, infinities, unrecognized, alive.

"Realism has no place in publishing." Next time someone tells you they're a realist, tell them publishing is the business of dreamism then slap them in the face with your Michael Jackson glove. Remember the maniacal girl in *2666* who said only storms and the Aztecs were real. I'm starting to understand what she meant.

I was afraid everyone was going to think I was just sharing transmissions from the dark part of the machine. I was afraid I'd sound like a man at confession. I was afraid I'd erase me, that some imaginary canopy I'd worked so hard to build would come crashing down, or it wouldn't. But once I was standing at the podium, alone with the spotlight blinding me, faces blurring into those floating electric seahorses you see from staring at the sun, I wasn't afraid of any of those things anymore — I was just afraid.

At the end of the poem where you die in the backseat of a rental car and I die wrapped in a huge tropical leaf, it happened. The shame came. So long little levee. I didn't cry, but my voice wavered then collapsed, like a video of engineers testing a bridge. It had nothing to do with us dying or our friends and family turning into wind, it was the part where I lied, the part where I said we'd never be forgotten by anyone ever again.

Today at work, I had to look up the definition for "poetry." Which was like a metaphor for a metaphor. I felt my face flush with heat. It wasn't shame or fear, it was more like I was about to read the definition of my own life. *Merriam-Webster* defines it as **1a:** metrical writing: verse; **b:** the productions of a poet: poems. It was, like all things, a disappointment. But after thinking about it, I realized that **b:** definition is perfect. After all, it is what *this* is. Also, technically, the shit I just took was poetry.

I was serious about that shit. Since language was invented, man has been trying to explain the feeling of taking a shit. I don't know why, but I know there is something inside us, something we want out. I'm talking about evil.

I've been thinking about suicide. This is a good thing—it's green tea, honey, clove. Thinking about suicide is the ultimate act of the ego. A form of dreaming. A detoxification. A release valve for responsibility. A narrative in which the best part is when you publish all my books and people start paying attention—a story where all is not lost.

There is this scene at the end of Season 5 of *The Wire* where out of nowhere Namond is arguing about AIDS in Africa as a member of his high school debate team. I couldn't stand where the writers went with this, it's not that it was too easy or the redemption angle was overwrought, it was more the lack of gray scale. Truth is, I never had that much sympathy for Namond's character, but for some reason, seeing him up at that podium, reciting all those AIDS statistics, I started to cry and I couldn't stop.

I am in the Sonora desert. I am here to bury my grand-mother on top of a mountain. Maybe it's a metaphor. "Waiting for the other shoe to drop," she used to say when I was a kid, and I had no clue what she was talking about. She spent her last three days alive on a gurney in the living room of the house where she was born, all her children gathered around her, crying, broken and brave. Waiting for her to die I had this revelation, or maybe it was after she died, that there is no other shoe, just the one we already have, and waiting.

The sky has no clouds here. Just a ridiculous blue. Never ending. In this way, it is more like an ocean than a sky. That wasn't the only revelation I had: life is a series of misunderstandings, leading to some final truth, unknowable... a single wave, separated from its source, alone, longing for a place to break—to call home.

It's like when you said a field of poppies and I thought you said a field of opposites. That's what a death is—a perfect misunderstanding.

Have you ever heard the coyotes call? When I was in Arizona, sleeping with the French doors open at the foot of Camelback mountain, in the middle of the night, I heard them. I thought I must be dreaming, it sounded like a mass murder, or perhaps a prison break, a series of high-pitched yips, yelps, and howls, from the long rising and falling moans, to the short, shrill yi-yis, a pack in heat or longing or mourning, howling and cackling and wailing and laughing and arguing and throwing their voices and mimicking children or perhaps fighting over one, or the carcass of some fresh kill, a jackrabbit cracking, screaming, and gurgling, the sound of playing and fighting overlapping like a choir, like teenagers drinking beer and on fire, like desire could talk and its voice was coming from a radio in a pick-up truck parked in the desert, like the sound of every nightmare culminating in a storm, a cloud that made its way into my room, the coyotes circling me, dancing, bloody, starving, desperate, fucking perfect.

There are two stories regarding my uncles and the ducks. First, they lived on a compound at the edge of the Sonoran dessert. There was a crude fence and shit in the yard. To feed the ducks, they would dumpster-dive. One of the all-time jackpots was the grapes. Red, full, king-of-France type grapes. After an hour, my uncle noticed one of the ducks had fallen down. Shortly after, all the ducks started dropping. Except one, that held on then finally succumbed. They did what you do when you kill all your ducks, they sat down in the white noise of guilt and said nothing. Tony decided they should pluck the ducks for their down. Edward explained how bad an idea this was. After a few minutes, Tony burst through the door like a kind of electricity and said, holy shit, one of the ducks had resurrected. One by one, the ducks, with trouble, as if coming out of a long sleep, slowly rose up, and in the bliss of remembering nothing, wobbled off into the yard.

This is not the poem about the ducks. This is about the night my uncle died. Randy Savage was fighting the Honky Tonk Man—the Hart Foundation ganged up on Macho Man as Honky Tonk pushed Miss Elizabeth then smashed his guitar over Macho Man's head while the Hart Foundation pinned down his arms. The night of no-longer-waiting. Sold-out Hershey Park Arena. The Saturday Night Main Event. The crowd going wild. Deafeningly alone.

When "Macho Man" Randy Savage died, obviously I thought of my grandmother. I saw her, 92 years old, just two days after her husband died, in the stands of a Mexican wrestling match in west Phoenix, the only gringo in the goddamned gym, booing and hissing on cue, rooting on the masked hero, my adopted brother Louis, "El Carcelero!," tears welling in her eyes, at this, the happiest moment of her life.

My nieces asked me where the soul is and I haven't been the same since. Instead of a raise, my job offered to get me a new chair in the form of one of those giant exercise balls. As if I don't realize they are actually saving money by buying me a plastic ball for a chair. They probably read some study saying how these things increase productivity and alertness, like how the entire workforce has had coffee shoved down their faces since the 80s. But I took it. Those things are supposed to really strengthen your core.

I've been thinking about how to end this book. You're right, that last poem about the plastic ball and the soul can't be the end. Not that Mylar doesn't capture the ethos of what we're after. The perfect way to say hope and despair at the same time. Fuck acceptance. At least the kind that anyone could ever know about. I want to say knife, and you start to bleed. I want to say what Nicanor Parra says after every reading: *I take it all back*. Maybe we should accept it—this book will never end.

Remember when we met in Philadelphia so I could save your life. Remember when we drove to some dinner to get a weird beer and a coffee each. Remember when Cori and Paige got out of the SUV and walked across the parking lot as we sat in the back, locked-in from the inside. Helpless, humiliated, at the mercy of. Remember how in that moment, relegated to mere characters of our own lives, we heard the voice-over of an omnipotent narrator sum it all up: *As adults looked on.*

"It's 89 degrees and I'm packing everything I own into my shitty Civic and driving to New Orleans. I pawned my guitars and TV and sold all my furniture, including my shower curtain, to the dude I buy pot from. Last week, he proposed to his lady while standing in a Toys 'R Us parking lot, his arms full of Marvel Universe action figures that he'd just shoplifted. Yes, Sampson, sometimes your dreams come true and you don't even know it."

You would have loved the young, drunk, impossibly-French girls at the party telling us about getting stuck in a private elevator, how it was like a horror movie, how the girl in New Jersey on the other end of the emergency intercom said, sorry there was nothing she could do and left them there, how they got that bitch fired a few days later, how it wouldn't have been that bad if there were some mirrors in there. Then they warned us not to dream of a giant vagina with teeth, that whatever we dreamed on our first night in our new apartment would come true. Turns out, I didn't dream anything that night, just the black nothingness of sleep. Wonder what that means?

I'm in the security line at JFK and they just piped Prince's "Let's Go Crazy" through the loudspeakers, and now it's Billy Idol's "Dancing with Myself." Who could calculate the residual damage of such events, but what I can tell you, as I take off my New Balances and place them on one of those plastic trays—I could stay here forever. There is a point when we all must accept that there is nothing but life and death and Tom Hanks' movies.

I went to the ER again. Concussed. I kept saying that word over and over in my head. When they asked me how I felt, I was a child whose toy was floating towards the deep end. Dumb, groggy, dull, angelic if you ask me. I just sat there like a broken Ken doll. Deep in what Rumsfeld called our "unknown unknown's," which is not too far from Keats' negative capability. When you have no choice, there's nothing to do but wade around in those unknowns like a child in a kiddy pool, unafraid of what's contained. I know you think I'm getting these head injuries just to get poems out of them. To each his own.

Depression is the fog that settles over the swamp you call your life. I hate to use metaphors but if I just tell you that I'm scared and guilty and angry and full of self-loathing all the time, is it even writing anymore? Maybe if I threw up pints of blood and passed out on my porch in my work clothes waiting for someone to find me the way my dad did when he was a little older than I am now, and maybe if that person who found me was you, then I wouldn't need to write to you anymore.

Remember when you drew the AWESOME card. Remember when Bill Murray was the right answer over Captain Kirk and you didn't flinch. Remember how nothing trumps *blowjobs & shampoo*. Remember when we covered your hairless body in magic-marker tattoos. The red MC Escher staircase on your neck. The three baby owls like a family on your forearm. Remember when I drew a black tornado over your heart. Desire gyre. Remember the next morning, in the shower, how you scrubbed and scrubbed and scrubbed, but you couldn't come clean.

Today is the day I am supposed to hear back about the job. I feel like my insides are made of confetti, or will implode like one of those buildings that conveniently caves-in on itself as a crowd of people with nothing better to do than watch behind yellow tape, or whatever it's called when all of the air comes screaming out of a balloon and the balloon flies around the room, puttering, panicked, rapidly growing smaller, until there's no more air left and it crashes to the ground, a puddle of bright-colored plastic campaigning for the single saddest thing in the universe. Why do the best things never have names?

I told my mom I'm scared because I put all my eggs in
one basket. She said all you can do is put all your eggs
in one basket, that there is always only one basket. She's
right, life is like Mickey Rourke — have you seen his face
lately — the secret of the world lies inside it. I'm telling you
this shit isn't skin, it's Mylar.

Today they're firing the quiet little gray-haired proofreader who happens to be the lead singer for the Sic F*cks. I can't help thinking about him breaking into song, screaming *Chop Up Your Mother*, spit flying in their faces, as scantily-clad nuns with bright red lipstick and torn stockings stand behind him rhythmically chopping Viking battle axes and giant butcher knives, while the bosses sit horrified behind their desks. He told me the difference between his generation and our generation is they either died young or remain best friends, a kind of family, and still get together and play music and drink and watch each other's kids grow up and go to college, while our generation just floats apart, slowly loses touch, gets different friends, different scenes, and eventually lets go. He tells me he still gets together every once in a while with the old CBGB crew on Bowery and that I should stop by. But all I can think is that I hope we die before we float apart.

Did I ever tell you about the time I walked into my boss's office — her prosthetic leg lying on the table like a recently-diffused bomb. Her face looked like a teenager whose mom just caught them masturbating. I wanted to run, but in a gesture of pure composure or embarrassment, she told me to sit down, the leg between us like an answer. I asked some stupid question but don't remember what it was, just time fucking up, forgetting to do whatever it does.

I've been trying to write to you, but find myself stuck in one of life's caesuras. Maybe away from the edge of any abyss, there is nothing to write about. No one to save. But even I know that's bullshit. I am made of lies instead of atoms. I'm afraid if I were to even sneeze, a billion of them, of me, would burst into the air — an ideal disease.

All nightmares are a matter of proportion. This is not wisdom, this is about having giant fucking hands, big as boats, unable to open doors that crush everything they touch. I'm trying to tell you something but the writing keeps getting in the way. Our love ricochets off earth, but we go on. I want to help you, I want to open you up and fix all the black and bloody shit in there. We are small, but so is the world. Also, there is hope.

ACKNOWLEDGEMENTS

Many thanks to the editors of the following journals in which these poems originally appeared:

Absent, Action Yes, Best American Poetry (online), Coconut, Death Hums, Ekleksographia, ESQUE, Fence, Forklift, Ohio, Free Verse, Glitterpony, Indigest, La Petite Zine, LIT, MiPoesias, New York Quarterly, No Dear, No Tell Motel, NOÖ Journal, Notnostroms, Octopus, Open Letters Monthly, Pax Americana, Poets for Living Waters, RealPoetik, SCUD, The Day Lady Gaga Died: an Anthology of NYC Poetry of the 21st Century, Sink Review, SIR!, Sixth Finch, Tarpaulin Sky, The Tusculum Review, and Typo.

Thanks to these small presses for publishing chapbooks in which a number of these poems appeared: Horse Less Press (*The Photograph*), Rope-a-Dope Press (*City of Moths*), Immaculate Disciples Press (*The Heart Is Green from So Much Waiting*) and Greying Ghost Press (*Self Help Poems*). Additional thanks goes out to Brave Men Press who originally published "XXIX" as a limited-edition coinside.

Thanks to Elisa Gabbert, Ana Božičević (qua, qua!), Julia Cohen, Dan Magers, Emily Frey, Kaveh Bassiri, Doug Hahn, Minal Singh, Rauan Klassnik, Amy Lawless, Ed Park, Ben Mirov, Ben Kopel, Ben Pease, Caroline Gormley, Jon-Michael Frank, Michael Johnson, Joseph Silvers, Mathias Svalina, and Matthew Henriksen for your help in making these poems.

Thanks to Matt Bollinger for the cover and back cover art, you are a genius, and to Mike Newton for the interior layout (the soul) of the book. Thanks to my friends who made the interior cover art: Bianca Stone, Eric Amling, Jonathan Marshall, and Sommer Browning.

Thanks to Jared White for writing the introduction and for just being Jared White.

To all my friends, you are my life…I carry you with me at all times like a book that saves me just by knowing it's there.

To my family, thank you for making me and everything that came after.

To my BIRDS: Justin Marks, Matt Rasmussen, Chris Tonelli, and especially my editor, Dan Boehl, where it all started sitting in the grass in Roanoke, Virginia reading each other poems at the edge of the world: NEVER-ENDING LOVE.

To, for, after, in, because, straight-through my love, Paige Taggart. Thank you for your made-up languages, impromptu songs, and strange ways of moving — you are a freak of love, friendship, and light.

This book is dedicated to my uncle, Tony Newhall.

Thomas Anthony Newhall, 1/30/1950 – 12/?/1987

Sampson Starkweather was born in Pittsboro, North Carolina. He is a founding editor of Birds, LLC. He lives in Brooklyn, NY, with the escape artist, Paige Taggart.

INDEX OF FIRST LINES